IN THE TEMPLE OF A PATIENT GOD
SABIR TANRISININ TAPINAĞINDA

Bejan Matur

In the Temple of a Patient God

SABIR TANRISININ TAPINAĞINDA

ཀ

Translated by Ruth Christie
Introduced by Maureen Freely

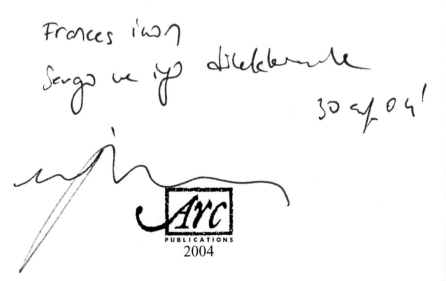

Frances iwon
Sergo ve iyo dileklerinle
30 ey 04'

ARC
PUBLICATIONS
2004

Published by Arc Publications,
Nanholme Mill, Shaw Wood Road
Todmorden OL14 6DA, UK

Design by Tony Ward
Printed at Antony Rowe Ltd.
Eastbourne, East Sussex

ISBN 1 900072 96 3

Some of these translations were first published
in the following journals:
Grand Street No. 70; *Near East Review* Vol. 2 No. 1;
Leviathan Nos. 4 & 5; *Agenda Modern Turkish
Poetry* Vol. 38 Nos. 3-4; *Acumen* No. 47.

The cover design is reproduced from a tülü (a shaggy-
pile Turkish rug with a simple and rather rough struc-
ture, soft to touch) with a design containing a series of
niches. Although reminiscent of a mosque, these niches
are probably associated to a much earlier cultural theme,
the Mother Goddess of Anatolia, divinity of the most
ancient neolithic Anatolian populations.

The publishers acknowledge
financial assistance from
ACE Yorkshire

**Arc Publications: 'Visible Poets' series
Editor: Jean Boase-Beier**

CONTENTS

from SONS REARED BY THE MOON (2002)

from IN HIS DESERT (2002)

SERIES EDITOR'S NOTE

There is a prevailing view of translated poetry, especially in England, which maintains that it should read as though it had originally been written in English. The books in the 'Visible Poets' series aim to challenge that view. They assume that the reader of poetry is by definition someone who wants to experience the strange, the unusual, the new, the foreign, someone who delights in the stretching and distortion of language which makes any poetry, translated or not, alive and distinctive. The translators of the poets in this series aim not to hide but to reveal the original, to make it visible and, in so doing, to render visible the translator's task too. The reader is invited not only to experience the unique fusion of the creative talents of poet and translator embodied in the English poems in these collections, but also to speculate on the processes of their creation and so to gain a deeper understanding and enjoyment of both original and translated poems.

Jean Boase-Beier

"I write the poetry of the steppes." Bejan Matur

One day in July 2000 a petite, dark-eyed, chic young woman stood on my doorstep, bringing me a copy of the first book of her poems published in Turkey: I immediately read the leading poem which gave the volume its title – *Rüzgar Dolu Konaklar* – (literally Wind-full Mansions).

I found this long poem in sixteen parts magical, mysterious and intriguing, puzzling too, and I had never read anything like it. It seemed to be a narrative, but of what nature? Part fairy-tale, folk-tale, mythical, even biblical; episodic, timeless, set in a locality somewhere in Eastern Turkey, among 'copperpots and kilims'.

There was an epic quality in the fated sufferings of a family, in the rugged stony landscape, in the journeys, in the repetitive lines like a chorus and in the rhythms of the original Turkish with subtexts of ritual and violence. Perhaps the best way to know a poem is to attempt a translation, so I began my journey with Bejan Matur which has continued for three years.

The title of this first poem was a predominant concern through out its translation. A title is often determined at the end of a translation, inner events of the poem guiding the choice. In the case of 'Winds' (as it came to be known familiarly in my household) the choice was not easy. 'Windswept' suggested the exteriors of lonely habitations on hills, a sort of Middle East *Wuthering Heights*, whereas the poet intimated mansions full of winds *howling* within and without. 'Windy Mansions' was considered but dropped as being too reminiscent of Forster's gentle mockery of names from Surrey stockbrokers' homes. Her wind is not domesticated. So in the final solution the translator opted for a freedom of translation, and 'Winds Howl through the Mansions' was the result.

Turkish is a language rich in proverbs and lively idioms. But it may be that the language reforms legalized by Ataturk's Assembly in the early decades of the twentieth century, although they led to greater literacy and brought the written language closer to the colloquial, also resulted in a depleting of Turkish vocabulary, rather as though the English language had outlawed all words rooted in Greek or Latin. Language became less grand, less rich, more demotic. The vacuum left by the purifying process of stripping away many of the Arabic and Persian words which had been there for a thousand years, has later been filled by foreign imports, particularly French. Writers and poets have always found a way to slip through or round impositions on language and Bejan, who belongs to a generation which forges its own language from old and new, has created a tongue of overpowering strength and beauty.

As there are many more English words which correspond to one of Turkish, the translator of Turkish into English must make decisions depending on context, mood and tone. Turkish has one phrase for the 'smell' of a rose, but in English this can be rendered by 'scent', 'perfume', 'fragrance': all have slightly different associations. In this field translation is bedevilled by choices and judgements.

A first reading of Bejan's poems is like drinking a glass of cool clear water – the words are so simple, elemental really.

> Wheat in our fields
> bitter water in our well.
> We dug earth's womb
> and gave it our language.
> ('Lament')

Lines are short and terse, complete in themselves, but at this point the reader / translator finds that the apparent simplicity masks, in the words of Jean Boase-Beier, "the strange, the unusual, the new". The concrete lies side-by-side with the abstract, the everyday with the enigmatic.

> I saw Allah. He was waiting in a hollowed-out tank.
> I entered the darkness of his soul and sat down.
> ('Talking with God')

> She keeps waiting for a voice
> from the fine-fingered fragrance of tobacco
> ('The Unhappy Queen')

For a translator the best strategy to convey the impact of such startling imagery was a rendering as literally direct as is possible from a source language that has case-endings and is

10

agglutinative, and consequently has a different word-order from English. No helpful conjunctions, no explanatory rearrangements, or 'poetic' turns of phrase from the translator. When unusual punctuation (or lack of it) pointed a sibylline finger either backwards or forwards, the ambiguity could be left to infiltrate the reader's imagination with its own mystery.

> I talked with them at a table
> shrouded in black, a bride adorned for death.
>
> ('Words')

> Phantoms crowd together
> in fear of eternity
> they build a city.
>
> ('The Virgin the Goddess')

I would like to mention here that I have adhered strictly to the punctuation of the original Turkish in the early long poem 'Winds Howl through the Mansions', but not elsewhere. Geoffrey Lewis has said in his book on Turkish grammar that there is no general agreement among Turkish writers or printers on how to punctuate.[1] Bejan's very individual style (lines invariably begin with a capital, sometimes few commas, or none at all, but decisive full-stops) has not always worked in English. The translations that follow the first long poem have tried to negotiate between adhering to the strict significance of the full-stop and as little other punctuation as possible.

The gnomic lines in Bejan's poems seem to be disconnected but leave the reader aware at some deeper level that fine invisible webs of thought and feeling have been spun. The poet clarified this for me when she explained her mode of composing. She cuts down her original version again and again, ten times if necessary, until language is pared down to the bone. The name of the game is reduction, not addition. She worked hard at the wordcraft and the translation has to strive to render the same naked, even bald, mystery.

Sound, rhythm and cadences (which may derive from Kurdish) are important to her and her creative process includes silent read-

---

[1] G. L. Lewis, *Turkish Grammar* (OUP, 1978), Section XXII, p. 276.

ings to herself, followed by reading aloud to small groups of friends, preferably those who do not write poetry, "because their perceptions of language are more objective and they can reveal their responses directly". She has often asked me to read aloud a line of translation while she gently marked out its rhythm by hand and wrist, and with unerring sensitivity suggested changes which have always been for the better.

The poet reveals two concepts of God in her work, 'Allah' and 'tanrı'. The god of Islam I have translated as Allah or God (upper case), 'tanrı' as the god or god (lower case). The latter is used regularly and idiomatically in a secular sense in modern Turkish although it has a very ancient mythological derivation, 'the sky-god'. But when Bejan Matur refers to 'the god' or 'god' she seems sometimes to be calling upon an older, pre-Islamic body of beliefs. At other times the reference is to her own idea of 'tanrı'. She has explained at some length her personal use of 'tanrı' in her poetry; a god she converses with, argues with, and calls to account, an equal god; not the god of monotheism but perhaps one of the pagan gods of a pantheist culture, "they come and go in my poetry". It may be worth noting that this concept of god seems to come very close to Jung's.

> It's pointless
> to hide my face from the god.
> ('The God at the Window')

I have been extremely fortunate in my contacts with Bejan Matur. So often she has been there in person to make suggestions and alterations. There have been e-mails too. I remember particularly a beautiful spring afternoon we spent working together in the Royal Festival Hall, overlooking the Thames, which glittered with light, life and movement. Water is one of the most frequent elements and metaphors in her work. I think that on that day the sight of it sustained us both visually and mentally, revitalizing the work.

I would like to express my gratitude to those at Boğaziçi University who sent Bejan Matur to me, to Prof. Saliha Paker's literary translation class of 2002 who gave helpful and interesting input to one of the longer poems; also to Selçuk and the Turkish friends of Bejan, in particular Algın and Kawa, who generously gave time and thought to reading some of the longer translations and explaining certain Turkish idioms; to Arc Publications and all who work there for producing this book, and as always to my husband, my stalwart consultant and word-processor.

I dedicate the translations to my grand-daughter Leah.

Ruth Christie

To read Bejan Matur is to walk into a windswept desert strewn with bones and broken bodies and stones stained red by absent gods. Nothing is whole; nothing explains itself; nothing lasts. Horsemen gallop out of the night only to fade into the mountains on the horizon. Gravestones line the roads. Ruined houses howl with wind while shepherds sing dirges about a shattered, scattered tribe left to wander in the dark.

It is a haunted, desolate and fragmented landscape in which every stone glows with a grief beyond words. One could say the same of the poems in this collection, and even of the poet herself. These are not autobiographical works: Matur is writing about a people not a person. Her poems are jagged shards that stand together only to expose history as a myth. But it is still possible to see them as children of her childhood. Matur comes from a Kurdish Alevi family and grew up in Southeastern Turkey at a time of virtual civil war.

And it is possible, when reading her poems, to imagine what that might mean. It is evident in their very shape, for Matur carves away at her images until she's stripped them down to the anguish at their heart. She claims no literary ancestors, drawing instead upon the oral traditions of her childhood. But there are shades of Blake in a poem like 'Children's Graves'. In six unassuming lines, it turns innocence into an epitaph:

So we died.
We slipped away out of darkness.
Beech trees saw us
and tiny stones.

Night and stars passed over us.
We were buried by the roadside. (p.103)

Beginning as it does *in medias res*, breaking off as it does in the middle of a thought, it calls to mind a page ripped from a book. We are never to know how these children died. Like everyone else in Matur's poetic world, they are buried with their secrets. The same might be said of her lexicon, which she has stripped down to the bare basics: stones and bones; caskets and shrouds;

fire and ice, eyes and severed heads, trees and temples, court-
yards and canyons, suns and moons and clouds and the never
dying wind, 'the good god of the steppes.' Matur uses the same
one-word images over and over, restlessly rearranging them as if
she, too, is trying to coax outside the spirits inside them. There
are times when she seems to be looking for her own soul:

> If the well had a tongue
> it would say
> that depth is a person searching the self,
> the gaze plunged within. (p.85)

When the well refuses to release its secrets, she moves on, seeking
solace, finding only new causes for grief. If the wind is the good
god of the steppes, she is their Emily Bronte, restlessly moving
about the ruins, calling to the dead: "Old as autumn / whispering
through the forest / the queen decays / in her black skirt of ice."
(p.59) Yet the gothic gloom she evokes is never final, for she senses
god in everything. And if god will not speak to her, that does not
stop her speaking to him: "I chased the severed head of my god /
from my house. / I addressed him straight and said, / Actually,
time that lies amongst these stones / means nothing. / It is our
unhappiness." (p.85)

In one of her most celebrated poems, 'To be in the world is
pain,' she remembers the kinder god of her childhood:

> When we are children, the god
> walks beside us.
> He touches our ear-rings
> and necklace.
> He enters and hides in our shiny shoes
> and the folds of our childish ribbon. (p.95)

It is almost as if her words are themselves gods, animating eve-
rything they inhabit. And here we come to the central paradox of
Matur's poetry. Matur does not write in Kurdish, the banned,
and therefore private, language of her early childhood. She writes
in Turkish, the language in which she was educated – one might
almost say exiled. The significance of this has not been lost on
her Turkish audience. When her readers have asked her to com-
ment on it, Matur has been circumspect. She talks on the one

hand of her fine education at a special lycee in Gaziantep, and of her Turkish being stronger than her Kurdish. And then she talks of the way in which dead languages lurk inside living languages. Words never forget their spiritual histories. She talks of Yeats, who wrote in English to invoke Irish. She talks of Andalucia, where Spanish still echoes Arabic. Echoing Lorca, she talks of unmasking and re-igniting folklore. She speaks of cutting her poems back and back, shaving them down to the bone until she has found the old word inside the new word, the Turkish poem that owes its haunting power to Kurdish.

So she is chipping and carving for a reason. Her dedication to this cause is absolute, and it takes her far beyond the questions raised by her own history. And it's this that makes her a world poet of the highest order. Indeed, there are echoes of Rilke in Matur's restless, relentless search for death in life and life in death:

> The virgin wanders in the courtyard,
> in the courtyard
> there are only eyes.
> She wishes
> for someone to look at her
> and understand
> she is searching for love in death.
> But no one looks
> as the weary heart
> flows away
> in the middle of
> the marble
> silent
> courtyard. (p.43)

Everywhere there are eyes, but no one looks. No one remembers and no one fights back: "Traces of blood, life leaking away. / Pouring from the memory of an ancient land, / mould enters the walls... / Every door waits for a neck / to be bowed in submission." (p.101). The ghosts of the recent past threaten to crowd in at such moments. Life is leaking away from her ancestral memories; in every house there is a neck bowing to the victors. There is an anger here that suggests an argument with the very traditions Matur is seeking to renew. But there is no fixed position. In

the opening passage of 'Wind Howls through the Mansion', it's
death that nurtures tradition and tradition that fends off death:

> When we were born
> It was our mother
> Who had caskets made for us
> And filled them with silver mirrors
> Dark blue stones
> And fabrics smuggled from Aleppo
> Later
> She would put us in those caskets
> And whisper in our ears
> Of roads
> And winds
> And mansions. (p.25)

The story the poet goes on to whisper in our ears is about a
family dispersed and destroyed, an exodus still in progress, a
woman uprooted but still clinging to the detritus of her lost home.
The modern nomad is Matur's great subject. Never able to look
forward without also looking back, never stopping anywhere for
long, she longs one moment for forgetfulness and the next mo-
ment for the truth:

> With the tremulous soul
> of all migrant peoples
> we peered about us.
> First at the mountains
> then the plain
> we peered at the rocks
> and the hot springs.
> We saw
> that nothing stirs
> from its bed.
> So then
> what curse
> what ill omen
> deceived us?
> What made the sky above us shrink
> To become our fate?
> …

Even the sinking sun
knew when to leave.
What are we waiting for?
How much longer will this last? (pp.47-9)

The story becomes more explicit in is 'The Island, Myself,
and the Laurel': "I went to the land of my kin / veiled in the
waters of a scattered womb, / spread under the sun to dry, their
hearts withered.... Unhappy glowering men / were peering /
among the stones. / Their land was full of broken bodies, / sev-
ered heads, unseeing eyes, / everything part of a mystery... / Is
this the proof of time, they ask, / that these broken bodies feel no
pain?" (p.81).

She belongs to a tribe, she says later, that has "nowhere to be
but words." And despite her best efforts, the words lead her
ever backwards: "The road we took back to the past / was be-
wilderment. / Everything we thought we found was childhood. /
A cool courtyard / and at the head of every street a well / each
lurking like a thief..." (p.87).

"I closed in on myself / with the single eye of an octopus. /
My body, my land / woke me to pain... / I was as scattered / as
the broken body of that land." (p.89). But inside those words hides
a gift, for it is the broken home and the broken body that sets the
imagination free. If a form is broken, then its spirit can escape.
Matur has a contempt for imposed order, a suspicion of temples,
forts, and just about anything that demands adulation:

No need for temples, I said.
This is simply a place.
The human soul must surely be a temple.
And rain the river of homelessness
reminds us of god and childhood. (p.113)

She is dismissive, too, of fixed traditions, even if these may be
her only links with her lost home: "Remember your ancestry, /
they say history will end / frozen in a photograph." (p.71). This,
she suggests, is cultural death: "Phantoms crowd together / in
fear of eternity / they build a city. / The city has graves." (p.41)
To stay alive, a tradition must be fluid: "History must move on / and
find its place. / The word must find its subject. / His hair must
grow long / And be damp and fragrant." (p.71). In the moveable

18

home she creates with her broken forms and re-ignited words, the poet engages with the gods inside them:

> Perhaps history is a mistake says the poet
> mankind's a mistake says god...

> And to correct his mistake
> he gives sorrow,
> only sorrow. (pp.65-7)

And it is to assuage this sorrow that the poet comes into her own.

Stripped as they are of all identifying marks, smooth and hard as stones, Bejan Matur's poems defy interpretation. When I first read 'Winds Howl Through the Mansions', the poem that opens this collection, I could hear the wind howling in my own head. But as I read on, I could not get past her poems' surfaces. I could fall in love with them, recite them, let them sink so deep into my imagination that I began to have nightmares about stones and severed heads, but still I couldn't understand them. It was only after I'd read them many times over that a moment arrived when I could just – and only just – see the world through their eyes.

There is no final epiphany in this world: no heaven, no redemption, no release from worldly sorrow. If there seems to be a line dividing the earth from the sky, the past from the present, the animate from the inanimate, the living and the dead, then it is the poet's job to break them down. It is through music and poetry that you begin to understand:

> The beauty of making mistakes
> and the peace of pain. (p.115)

Loneliness is not a cul de sac:

> Stones too need loneliness.
> And olive trees
> and the inside of houses where dark shadows lurk. (p.117)

There may be no escape from grief – "the death of my friend will be / the black shawl round my shoulders." (p.127). But – just as god gave us sorrow to make up for his mistake – Bejan Matur's

19

shiny, stony words help us understand why sorrow itself is never
a mistake:

> Darkness carries our destiny
> and makes us feel. (p.127)

Maureen Freely

IN THE TEMPLE OF A PATIENT GOD

SABIR TANRISININ TAPINAĞINDA

from
WINDS HOWL THROUGH THE MANSIONS (1996)

RÜZGÂR DOLU KONAKLAR

Doğduğumuzda
Bizim için yaptırdığı sandıklara
Gümüş aynalar
Lacivert taşlar
Ve Halep'ten kaçak gelen kumaşlar
Dolduran annemiz
Bir zaman sonra
Bizi koyup o sandıklara
Yol
Rüzgâr
Ve konakları fısıldayacaktı kulağımıza.
Yalnız kalmayalım diye karanlıkta
Çocukluğumuzu ekleyecek
Avunmamızı isteyecekti
O çocuklukla.
Sırtımızdan jiletle akıtılan kanın
Karıştığı uzun ırmağa
Bırakıldığımızda
Annemiz bu kadarını istemezdi

Bu yüzden
O uyurken
Uzaklaştık
Diyorduk sulara.
Gidişin kendisinden artakalan
Her şey, herkes burada.
Ben buradayım
Kardeşlerim yitikliğiyle burada
Annem elbiseleriyle
Erkek kardeşim savaş korkusuyla
Babam burada hiç uyanmış olmasa da
Dünya eksilmiş etrafımda
Bir düş sanki olanlar
Uzayan ve uzadıkça acıtan

24

WINDS HOWL THROUGH THE MANSIONS

When we were born
It was our mother
Who had caskets made for us
And filled them with silver mirrors
Dark blue stones
And fabrics smuggled from Aleppo
Later
She would put us in those caskets
And whisper in our ears
Of roads
And winds
And mansions.
To stop us being lonely in the dark
She would add our childhood too
To comfort us
With that childhood.
But when we were left
In the long river whose waters streamed
With blood that poured from ritual razor-slashes on our backs
Our mother never wanted such an outrage
And that is why
We kept telling the waters
While she was sleeping
We moved far away.

What's left from that flight
Everything, everyone is here.
I am here
My brothers and sisters are here with their loss
My mother with her dresses
My brother with his fear of war
My father's here but not awake
Around me the world has shrunk
All like a dream
The longer it lasts the more it hurts

I

Annemiz
Siyah kadife elbisesini okşadığında
Saçlarını düşürerek bakışlarına
Babamızı hatırlardı:

Beyaz bir dağda olduğunu söylüyordu onun
Beyaz ve her bahar küçülen bir dağda

II

Hepimizden büyük olan
Ve uzaktaki savaştan korkan
Erkek kardeşimiz
Dönmeyince bir daha
Biz de korktuk savaştan.
Ama savaş değildi onu bırakmayan.
Gelirken yanımıza
Atıyla uyumuş
Babamızın karşısındaki karlı dağda

Annemizin yüzü azaldıkça
Omuzları küçüldükçe annemizin
Şaşırdık hangi dağa bakacağımıza

III

Evimizin uzun sofasında
Kadife elbisesi uzayıp
Gümüş başlığı ağırlaştıkça
Bolardıkça gümüş kemeri
Annemiz benziyordu baktığı dağlara.
Baharda inceliyordu kabuğu
Ama ulaşamıyorduk ona.
Ölüyordu
Bu defa gerçekten eriyordu
Bir daha görünmedi sofada

I

Our mother
Stroking her black velvet dress
And veiling her gaze with her hair
Would remember our father:

She said he was on a white mountain
A white mountain getting smaller every spring

II

When our brother
Older than all of us
And afraid of the distant war
Never came home
We too feared the war.
But it wasn't war that kept him away.
On his way back
He fell asleep with his horse
On the snowy mountain facing our father's

As our mother's face grew thinner
And our mother's shoulders shrank
We wondered which mountain to look at

III

On the long veranda of our house
As her velvet dress grew longer
Her silver hairband heavier
Her silver belt looser
Our mother looked more and more
Like the mountains she watched.
In spring her shell was wearing out
But we couldn't reach her.
She was dying
This time pining away
She never appeared again on the veranda

IV

Her kış kaybolan
Ve baharda ortaya çıkan
Bir ağaç oldu annemiz

Dövmeleri olan bir meşeydi o
İniltisi geliyordu kulağımıza

V

Annemiz
Her gece siyah kadifesiyle
Dolaşıyordu dağların arasında
Kökleri olmayan bir meşeydi o
Suskun, arasıra ağlayan

Ayrılmadan daha
Toplaşır gölgesine annemizin
Fısıldaşırdık aramızda
Tanrım n'olur bağışla
Evimizi bağışla tanrım n'olur
Dokunma sofamıza
Orada gülebiliyoruz ancak
Orada adamakıllı susuyoruz
Orada ağzımız bizim oluyor
Dokunmasak da

Görüyoruz annemizi uzaktan

VI

Soğuklar başladığında
Atlılar gelmişti bizi almaya
Yaşlı ve tuhaf atlılardı
Korkutmuşlardı bizi
Kar yağmıştı bakışlarına.
Ve hiç konuşmadan bizimle
Bakmadan ellerimizin küçüklüğüne
Konaklara götüreceklerdi bizi
Rüzgârla uğuldayan konaklara

28

IV

Lost every winter
Returning in spring
Our mother became a tree

A tattooed oak
Her moaning in our ears

V

Every night
In her black velvet dress
Our mother wandered among the mountains
She was a rootless oak
Silent, now and then weeping

Before we parted
We would gather in our mother's shadow
And whisper among ourselves
Please God forgive us
Spare our house
Don't touch our veranda
Only there can we laugh
Only there can we be really silent
Only there can we say what we like
And even if we don't touch her

We can see our mother from afar

VI

When the cold spell began
Horsemen came to take us away
Horsemen old and strange
Who made us afraid
Snow fell on their gaze.
Without a word
Not looking at our little hands
They came to carry us off to the mansions
Mansions howling with winds

VII

Annemiz
Babamızın ve kardeşimizin ortasında
Usulca uyurken
Uzaklaştık yaşlı atlılarla.
Boynumuz ağrıdı geriye bakmaktan
Gözlerimiz uzadı her kıvrımda.
Ama boşuna
Boşuna bizim ağlayışımız
Hastalığımız boşuna
Yönü yitirmişti atlılar

Dönemedik bir daha

VIII

Dağlardan yuvarlanan taşlar gibiydik.
Dört kızkardeş
Gölgesiyle derinleşen bir vadide
Artık bizim olmayan
Yatağımızı aradık
Aradık yatağımızı günlerce.
Kaç dağ gittiysek
O kadar uzaktık birbirimizden
O kadar yalnız kendimizle

IX

Ne son ne başlangıç
Ne içeri ne dışarı
Oradaydık
O taştan dünyanın ortasında.
Yollarımız uzadıkça
Annemizin dövmeleri kararmakta

X

Ayrılacaktık herbirimiz
Bir yolağzında.

30

VII

While our mother
Slept peacefully
Between our father and brother
We went far away with the old horsemen.
Our necks ached with looking round
Our eyes narrowed at every bend.
But in vain
We wept in vain
Our sickness was in vain
The horsemen had lost the way

We could never go back

VIII

We were like rocks rolling from the mountains.
We four sisters
In a valley of deepening shadow
Searched for the beds
No longer ours
Searched for days.
With every mountain we crossed
We were so far from each other
So alone with ourselves

IX

No beginning no end
No inside no outside
There we were
In the midst of that world of stone.
As our paths lengthened
Our mother's tattoos grew darker

X

We would all separate
Where the road split.

Ama önce kim
Kim korkacaktı
Yoldan
Geceden
Ve yaşlı atlıdan.
Sıramız yoktu
Bu yüzden ürperiyorduk her ayrımda.

Ben kalmıştım sona
Önümde uzanan dar yolla
Acılarından güç alan
Bir yolcuydum artık hayatta

XI

Geldiğimde rüzgâr dolu ilk konağa
Günlerce uyudum
Kilimler ve bakırlar arasında.
Rüzgârı sevebilirdim
Kapılar ve pencereler olmasa

XII

On yılım geçti rüzgârla
Üşüdüm her konakta
Konuşmanın ne anlamı var diyordum
İnsanın yankısı olmazsa

Suskun konaklar gibiydim
Kapıları gittikçe çoğalan

XIII

Gümüşler ve atlar azaldıkça
Taşınıyordum oradan oraya
Yıldızların sesini tanıyordum
Güneye yaklaştıkça

XIV

Geceleri
Yalnız ve budala ay

But who would be the first
The first to be afraid
Of the way
The night
And the old horseman.
We were in no order
We trembled at every parting of the ways.

I was the last
The narrow road stretched before me
Gathering strength from their grief
I was the traveller

XI

When I came to the first windswept mansion
I slept for days
Among copperpots and kilims.
I could have loved the wind
But for the doors and windows

XII

Ten years I spent with the wind
I was cold in every mansion
There's no sense in talking I said
If there can't be a human echo

I was like the silent mansions
With more and more doors

XIII

As the horses grew fewer the silver less
I moved from place to place
As I neared the south
I recognized the voice of the stars

XIV

At night
The lonely foolish moon

Bana benziyordu
Bir tuhaflık vardı gülüşümde
Büyüyordum.
Aşkı düşünüyordum arasıra
Efendisini gövdenin.
Hangi gece uykusuz kalsam
Toprak kokuyordum

Ve çıktığım her yolculukta
Yorgunluğuma aldırmadan
Düşler kuruyordum.
Yolların korkutmadığı bir zamanda
Yoksulluğuyla alay eden
Yeşil gözlü bir adam çıktı karşıma
Gözleri koyulaştı adamın
Yaşlandıkça

XV

Çocuklarım oldu o yeşil gözlü adamdan
Biri askerdeyken, diğeri kızıl saçlı olan
İki oğlan.
Ve gelinim,
Her gece kızıl saçlı oğlumla uyuyan.
Üşürdü hep
"Yenge ayakların ne sıcak"
Derdi ona sokularak.
Onüç yaşında iki çocuk
Uyurlardı her gece fısıldaşarak.
O gecelerden birinde
Yağmur girmişti uykusuna.
Saçlarını bana bırak
Saçlarını bana bırak
Diyen yağmur,
Büyülemişti oğlumu uykuda.
Saçlarını rüzgârla yıkadığı
Tepeye çıktığımda
Görünen ova
Sular altındaydı
Bulutlar yapışmıştı toprağa.
Bir kıpırtı bekliyordum

Resembled me
There was something strange in my laugh
I was growing up.
Sometimes I thought about love
Lord of the body.
Nights when I couldn't sleep
I smelt of earth

And on every journey I took
I ignored my tiredness
And daydreamed.
Once when the roads no longer scared me
There came a green-eyed man
Who made fun of poverty
As he grew older
His eyes grew darker.

XV

I had children by that green-eyed man
Two lads
One joined the army, the other had red hair.
And my daughter-in-law,
Slept every night by my red-haired son.
He was always cold
'How warm your feet are'
He would say
As he pressed closer.
At thirteen the two children
Went to bed whispering together.
One night
Rain entered his sleep.
Leave me your hair
Leave me your hair
Said the rain
And cast a spell on my son in his sleep.
When I climbed the hill
Where he washed his hair with wind
The plain was under water
Clouds clung to the earth.
I was waiting for a movement

Bir ses
Oğlumu gizleyen sulardan.
Arkamda toplanan köylüler
Uçları yanan sopalarla
Karanlığı hatırlattılar bana.
Duramazdım
İndim buharlaşan toprağa.
Çamurlar arttıkça
Gücüm yetmiyordu karanlığa.
Üşümesinden korkuyordum yine
Saçlarının kirlenmesinden.
Bir ses
"Ölmüş" dediğinde
Üşümüyordu artık oğlum
Sessizdi yağmurdan.
Yüzüm çamurlu ve keder içinde
Taşıdım gövdesini,
Saçlarını taşıdım ellerimde.
Yüzükoyun bindirildiği at
Tepeyi çıkarken
Işık sızdırıyordu gizlice.

XVI

Yeşil gözlü adamın
Bıraktığı yatakta
Yaşlanıyorum tavana baktıkça.
Artık
Anneminki kadar uzun eteklerim.
Saçlarım uzun
Oğlumun kızıl saçlarından.

Kısa sürdü her şey
Yolculuklar
Ölüm
Ve konaklar
Hiçbir şey kalmadı etrafımda
İsten kararmış sütunlardan başka

Gücümü toplamalıyım son defa
Saçlarım kına kokmalı

A voice
From the waters hiding my son.
The villagers gathered behind me
With their flaming torches
Reminded me of the darkness.
I couldn't stay still
But went down to the steaming earth.
The mud grew deeper
I had no power against the dark.
I feared he'd be cold
And his hair dirty again.
When a voice said
'He is dead'
My son felt cold no longer
He was quieter than rain.
My face streaked with mud and grief
I carried his body,
I carried his hair in my hands.
They put him facedown on the horse
As it climbed the hill
It was secretly shedding light.

XVI

In the bed abandoned by the green-eyed man
I grow old gazing at the ceiling.
Now
My skirts are as long as my mother's.
My hair longer
Than the red hair of my son.

Nothing lasted long
Journeys
Death
Mansions
Around me nothing remained
But pillars dark with soot

I must gather my strength for the last time
My hair must smell of henna
There must be apple-blossom in the water

37

Elma çiçekleri olmalı suyumda.
Ve tanrı beni duyuyorsa
Daracık bir mezar istiyorum ondan
Konakların büyüklüğünü
Uğultusunu unutturan

YAŞLIKIZ TANRIÇA

Belki bu yüzden
Ayın sevgili tanrıçası Sin
Mabedini unuttu
Bu anlamsız boşlukta

Bu yüzden belki
Bin yıl uyudu insan
Ve uyandı sonunda.
Anladı
Bir uyku olduğunu varlığın
Ve cevapsız
O günden sonra.

Biliyorum orada
O ürkütücü başlangıçta
Bir şey bekliyor canlılar
Bir tufan olacak
Her şey toplanacak başlangıca

Oysa kapandı kapı
Âhı kaldı kalanların.
Üzerinde su gibi aziz yazan
Uğursuz beyaz taşlar
Bağlandı ölüme ve yalnızlığa

Yılın ilk gecesinde yaşlıkız
Annesiyle çıkıp
Yıldızların altında

That washes my dead body.
And if God can hear me
I ask for a narrow grave
To make me forget
Those spacious mansions
And their howling

THE VIRGIN THE GODDESS

Sin[1], beloved goddess of the moon
forgot her temple
in this meaningless void,
perhaps for the reason,

the reason perhaps,
that humanity slept for a thousand years
and at last woke up,
and understood
that existence was a sleep,
and had no answers
from that day on.

I know that there in that fearful beginning
the living are waiting for something.
There will come a flood
and all will assemble for the beginning.

But the door was closed.
Of those left, only sighs remained.
Ill-omened white stones,
inscriptions precious as water,
were bound to death and loneliness.

On the first night of the year the virgin
went out with her mother.
When she opened her hands

---

[1] *Sin* In Sumerian religion, god of the moon and father of the sun-god. Su-en
(contracted to Sin) designated the crescent moon.

Ellerini açtığında,
Yalvardığında aya ve yıldızlara
Tanrıça duymuştu onu
Fısıldamıştı Kays'la
Aşk kalbi korkuyla doldurur
Sırrı yok eder
Dokunur yalnızlığa

Bilmiyor tanrıça
Bu geçen zaman boyunca
Yaşlıkız inandı
Yüzünü sürdüğü taşlara.
Mağaralara inandı çok.
İnandı orada kaynayan suyun
İnsanı hayata bağlayacağına

Kapıları olsa da şehrin
Nefes olamıyor ona.

O gece uyumadı yaşlıkız
Aynada beyaz bir kadın
Bulmak umuduyla
Koştu sulara

Belki bir el
Aşka uzanan
Deliliğe
Gül kokusuna

Her şey
Her şey unutkan.
Şu savrulan
Küçük yaprak bile
Çıksa girdiği kuyudan
Başka bir şey olacak.
Ama olmuyor.
Sonsuzluk korkusuyla
Toplaşan görüntüler
Şehri kuruyorlar.
Mezarları oluyor şehrin.

beneath the stars
and pleaded with the moon and stars
the goddess heard her.
She whispered with Kays.[2]
And love fills the heart with fear,
destroys the mystery,
and touches loneliness.

The goddess does not know
that all this time
the virgin believed
in the stones she rubbed her face on.
And had great belief in caves.
She believed that the hot springs there
would bind a human to life.

Even if the city has gates
there is no air for her to breathe.

That night the virgin did not sleep
but ran to the waters,
hoping to find
a silver woman in her mirror.

Perhaps a hand
stretching out for love
for madness
for the fragrance of a rose,

everything,
everything is forgetful.
If even the little windblown leaf
comes out of the well it entered
it will be different.
But there's no change.
Phantoms crowd together
in fear of eternity
they build a city.
The city has graves.

---

[2] *Kays* Arabic poet under the name of Mecnun famous for his love of Leylâ.

41

Çocuk mezarlarında fulyalar açıyor
Yaşlılarınkinde zakkumlar

Her şey kendinin âhı
Toprak
Taş
Duvar.
Toprağı ve taşı
Göğe taşıyan duvar
Biliyor
Kulelere cevabı yok göğün,
Sonsuzluk ay gibi
Esirgiyor kendini dünyadan.

Yaşlıkızın da bildiği bir şey var
Çıkıp
Önünde bağıracağı bir duvar bulabilir.
Adı gibi mezar olan ne varsa
Sığınabilir onlara.
Başını vurabilir
O uğursuz beyaz taşlara

Vadedilmiş
Ve uzak her şey için
Bir çizgi oluyor ağzı
Göğsü doluyor
Sesini yitirmiş göğün
Uğultusuyla

Yaşlıkız dolaşıyor avluda
Avluda sadece
Gözler var.
İstiyor ki,
Aşkı ölümde aradığını
Anlayan biri varsa
Baksın ona.
Ama bakmıyor kimse.
Bakmıyor
Kalp yorulup
Boşalırken
Mermer
Suskun
Avlunun ortasına.

Jonquils open on children's graves,
oleanders on the graves of the old.

Everything grieves for itself,
earth,
stone,
wall.
The wall that lifts
earth and stone skywards
knows
the sky has no answer to the towers.
Eternity like the moon
keeps itself from the world.

There's one thing the virgin knows.
She can go and find
a wall to shout before.
Whenever there is a grave like her name
she can shelter there.
She can beat her head
on those ill-omened white stones.

For all those promises
far away,
her mouth narrows to a line.
Her breast fills
with the wuthering of a sky
that has lost its voice.

The virgin wanders in the courtyard,
in the courtyard
there are only eyes.
She wishes
for someone to look at her
and understand
she is searching for love in death.
But no one looks
as the weary heart
flows away
in the middle of
the marble
silent
courtyard.

YOLAĞIDI

I

Haritaları
Taşınmayacak kadar büyük olan
Adamlar
Koklayarak buldular yolu.
Soyun devamı
Ateşin
Ve suyun
Başı için

II

Bozkırın iyitanrısı rüzgâr
Göğsümüzden geçerek
Kutsadı bizi

III

Ateş yakmayı bilmeyen el
Tanrının üzerine olsun.

Şu doğan günün başı için
Diyordu annem
Şu doğan günün
Üzümün
Ve buğdayın
Sabrı için

IV

Ateşi tanıyan el
Suyla yıkanan göz gibiydi gece.
Geldik
Ve sığındık ovaya.
Tarlamızda buğday
Kuyumuzda acı su.
Kazdık rahmini toprağın,

LAMENT

I

Men
their maps
too big to carry
followed their noses
and found the way.
For the sake
of fire
of water
and the survival of the tribe.

II

Wind the good god of the steppe
blew through our hearts
and blessed us.

III

It must be a supergod's
the hand that can't light a fire.

For the sake of daybreak
my mother would say,
for daybreak
and the patience
of grape
and wheat.

IV

Night was like an eye washed in water
and the hand that knew fire.
We came
and sheltered in the plain.
Wheat in our fields
bitter water in our well.

Dilimizi verdik ona.
Bir ürpermeyle yitirdik aşkı
Yanmış o konağın kıyısında.
Yerle gök arasında tereddüt kuşlar,
Artık mümkün olmayacak soyun devamı
Diyerek uçtular.
Kuşlara inandık.
Soyun devamı olmayacak
Diyen telaşa.

V

Göçle gelen
Her kavmin
Titrek ruhuyla
Bakındık etrafa.
Önce dağlara
Sonra ovaya
Taşlara bakındık
Kaynayan suya.
Gördük ki,
Hiçbir şey kıpırdamıyor
Yatağında.
O zaman
Hangi lanet
Hangi âh
Girdi kanımıza.
Neydi başımızda daralan göğü
Yazgımız yapan.

VI

Yapraklar gözleridir meşenin
Diyenlerin ardından
Tanrımız da
Gizlendi mağaraya

Oradan üfledi ölümü
Denizin dibindeki karanlıktan.

We dug earth's womb
and gave it our language.
We lost love with one shudder
on the edge of that charred mansion.
Birds hovered between earth and sky.
Now the tribe cannot possibly survive
they said and flew away.
We believed the birds
in their flurry,
that the tribe would not survive.

V

With the tremulous soul
of all migrant peoples
we peered about us.
First at the mountains
then the plain
we peered at the rocks
and the hot springs.
We saw
that nothing stirs
from its bed.
So then
what curse
what ill omen
deceived us?
What made the sky above us shrink
to become our fate?

VI

After they said
that leaves are the eyes of the oak-tree
our god too
hid away in the cave.

From there he blew death
from darkness in the depths of the sea.

VII

Şu batan gün bile
Gideceği zamanı bildi
Biz neyi bekliyoruz
Ne kadar sürecek daha

VIII

Vakti geldiğinde
Gitmek kadar iyi olan ne varsa
Girdi uykumuza.
Kadına inandık
Soyun devamı olmayacak
Diyen bakışına.

IX

Kadındım o zaman
Bulaşmamıştım
Cinslerin o tuhaf karmaşasına

Titreyerek sevdiğim her şey
Kesti kanımı
Gönül düşürdüğüm her şey kırılgan

X

Anladım
Zaman geçiyor
Ne gitmek, gitmek olacak
Ne kalmak

Sağır dilsizlerin
Diliyle gelip
Sözü düşünsem
Yerim olmayacak

VII

Even the sinking sun
knew when to leave.
What are we waiting for?
How much longer will this last?

VIII

When the time came
all the good things like leaving
entered our sleep.
We believed the woman
and her eyes that said
the tribe would not survive.

IX

I was a woman then.
I'd never been involved
in the strange complexities
of gender.

Every tender loving
cut off my blood
everything I loved was fragile.

X

I understood
time passes.
Going is not going
nor staying, staying.

If I come with the language
of the deaf and dumb
and think of words
I'll have no place to be.

XI

Ama ruhum
Ruhum başındayken yolun
Safça inandı toprağa

Kadına inandı
O saflık uykusuna

XII

Rüyada
Sol kolum kırılsa
Çocukluğum

Su uykulu
Su dalgın
Aşktan

XIII

Toprak iyidir
Acıyı çeker
Diyor annem.
Kınalı saçlarıyla kapatıldığı ev,
Yanmış.
Ama gözleri,
Bazı geceler dağınık duran
Yıldızlara benziyor. Hareli.
Elleriyse toprak kokuyor.
Bunu tuhaf bulduğumda
Bana dokunsun istiyorum
Rahatlatmıyor.

XIV

Anladım zaman geçiyor
Anne olmak acısını anlamak başkalarının
Ve merak uyandırdığında gelir bahar

XI

But my soul,
my soul at the start of its journey
in its purity believed the earth,

believed the woman
and that sleep of innocence.

XII

If my left arm is broken
in the dream
it is my childhood

water sleepy
water dreamy
from love.

XIII

Earth is good
my mother says,
it takes away pain.
The house that enclosed her with her henna'ed hair,
burned down.
But her eyes, hazel with green motes
are like those nights of scattered stars.
And her hands smell of earth.
When I find this strange
I want her to touch me
but it doesn't soothe my pain.

XIV

I understand time passes.
To be a mother is to know the pain of others.
When the sense of wonder starts, it's spring.

Bense bir kış resmi içinde ilerliyorum
Yolumda selviler
İstasyon bekçisinin mutsuz karısı
Umudum uzakta
Güneşin acıtıp, emdiği karda

XV

Bakışım yumuşadı sonra
Taş avluda açan begonya
Pamukta oynaşan titrek beyaz
Güneşe akar ne varsa

XVI

Çığlık çığlığa kuşlar
Vadiye doluşunca
Anne oldum
Seviştim bir adamla

XVII

Resm içinde dalgın
Bekler
Olgunlaşır
Çürür zaman.
Putlara sövmeli
Putlara sövmeli
Daha ne kadar

XVIII

Su: Ölü yağmur
Kalır kuyusunda rahmin
Soyumuz sürmedi
Tükendi.

There I am setting out in a winter scene
cypresses on my road
the unhappy wife of the station-master
my hope far away
in snow sucked dry hurt by the sun.

XV

My look softened later
in the stone courtyard the begonia opening
the quivering playful white in the cotton,
everything flows into the sun.

XVI

When screeching birds
filled the valley
I became a mother
made love with a man.

XVII

In the picture
time dreams
and waits
ripens
and rots.
This swearing at idols
this cursing of idols
how much longer?

XVIII

Water: dead rain
remains in the well of the womb
our tribe did not survive
it came to an end.

ACIMIZI EMİYOR AY

Hüseyin Kendal için

I

Ve sesler topladık her taraftan
Balkonlardan mandolin sesleri
Kahkaha sesleri odalardan
Buğudan yosundu dudaklarımız
Susuyorduk durmadan

Kaya diplerinden akan sular gibiydik
İçli ve alıngan

Ne sorumuz vardı soracak hayata
Ne de cevabımız bakışlarımızdan başka

Bazı geceler büyüyen ayla bulduğumuz yol
Dağlara çekiyordu gövdelerimizi
Dağlara parçalanmaya

II

Çocukluğumuzun
Parıltılı gözlerini özleyen vadiler
Gözlerimizi istiyordu
Bırakmamızı istiyordu gözlerimizi
Hiç ağlamadan.
Ağlamadık hiç
Bıraktık gözlerimizi
Şarkılarımızı da

III

Artık yabancıydı bize bu kara.
Bulutların bulanık kederiyle yüklüydük
Yağacağı toprağı olmayan.
Yorgunduk
Bir esinti bekliyorduk yaralarımıza.

THE MOON SUCKS UP OUR GRIEF
for Hüseyin Kendal

I

We gathered sounds from everywhere
the sound of mandolins from balconies
the sound of laughter from rooms
our lips mossy with damp
we stayed endlessly silent.

We were water hiding under steep cliffs
shy and touchy

We had no questions to ask of life
no answers but the glances we exchanged.

Some nights as the moon grew big
the path we took
drew our bodies to the mountains
to the mountains to be dispersed

II

The valleys that longed for the shining eyes
of our childhood
asked for our eyes
asked us to leave our eyes behind
without tears.
We never cried.
We left our eyes behind
and our songs.

III

This land was strange to us now.
Laden with turbid clouds of grief
but no rain-soaked earth.
We were tired
waiting for a breath of air on our wounds.

Zeytin ağaçları bizi bekliyordu
Bizi bekliyordu
Adsız böcekleriyle beyaz topraklar.

IV

Artık tanrımız yoktu
Unutulmuştuk.
Derinlerde bırakmıştik bakışımızı
Görmüyorduk.
Ne anılarımız bekliyordu bizi
Ne de geçerken iz bırakıyorduk
Sanki o an orada yaratılmıştık
Dünya buhardandı bizse acıdan

V

Acımızı emerek büyüyen ay
Her nasılsa bekliyordu uzakta.
Yürüyorduk ayın acıyı örten dokunuşlarıyla.
Ama yorgunduk hâlâ,
Çıkamıyorduk makilerin fısıldayan yaprakları arasından
Uzanıp dinlenmeliydik
Unutmalıydık mandolin düşlerimizi
Ellerimizi yatırmalıydık buhara
Bastırmalıydık kederimizi göğsümüzde açılan boşluğa.
Mandolin telleriyle
Derinleşen parmaklarımıza dokunan rüzgâr,
Bir rüzgâr kalmıştı tanıdık olan
Ona bırakmalıydık kendimizi
O her şeyi bilen
Her şeyi götüren rüzgâr

Rüzgârdı dokunuşlarıyla parçalarımızı toplayacak olan

The olive trees were waiting
and the white earth with its nameless insects
were waiting for us.

IV

Now we had no god.
We were forgotten.
We had left behind our gaze
in the depths
we could not see.
No memories waited for us
nor did we leave any trace as we passed
as though we had been created then and there
the world of vapour and we of grief.

V

As it sucked up our grief the waxing moon
was waiting somewhere far off.
We walked with touches of the moon
veiling our pain
but we were still tired
we could not emerge from the whispering leaves of the maquis.
We had to lie down and rest
we had to forget our mandolin-dreams
we had to lay our hands to rest on the vapour
and impress our grief on the opening void of our hearts.
The wind at our fingers
deepened by the mandolin strings,
the familiar wind that lingered,
we had to give our selves
to the wind that knew all
the wind that carried all away

One touch of that wind would gather up our remains.

MUTSUZ KRALİÇE

Etekleri buz tutmuş
O mutsuz kraliçe
Artık inanmıyor
Gözün büyüsüne

Günlerdir beklediği ses
Gizlenmiş tepelerin ötesine

Arasıra buluşup
Kervanların sığacağı darlıktaki
Sokaklardan sözeden adam artık yok
Anlayan yok
Baharat satılan hanların
Kokulu yalnızlığından

Bir ses bekliyor ısrarla
İnce parmaklı tütün kokusundan

Ormanda fısıldayan
Güz kadar yaşlı kraliçe
Dökülüyor
Buzdan ve siyah eteğiyle

AN VE MASAL

Güneşin ve suyun tadıyla
Uçunca bulutların tarlasına
Orada gece yok
Gece olmuyor uzaklarda

Boynumda gümüş bir kafes
Sadakatsiz bir cariye gibi
Uzanıp kıvrıldım ayın ortasına
O bir dede

THE UNHAPPY QUEEN

Her skirts turned to ice
the unhappy queen
no longer believes
in the eye's magic

the voice she awaited for days
hidden beyond the hills.

Now there's no one to describe
the narrow alleys where sometimes the caravans meet
and squeeze past
no one who knows
the perfumed loneliness
of spice-selling hans.

She keeps waiting for a voice
from the fine-fingered fragrance of tobacco.

Old as autumn
whispering through the forest
the queen decays
in her black skirt of ice.

THE MOMENT, THE LEGEND

I flew into the field of clouds
with the taste of sun and water
there is no night there,
there's no night at the ends of the earth.

Bound in a silver cage
like a faithless concubine,
I curled up into the moon,
the moon a grandfather

Ben tanrıça
Günlerce uçtuk alacakaranlıkta

Boynum ince
Kalbim boş
Sürdüm yüzümü ağaçlara
Rüzgâra sürdüm gözlerimi acıyla
Geçtiğim yollar
Ve uçtuğum
O gecesiz gökyüzü
Bulutların tarlasında oturan
Tanrı kadar yorgun
Fısıldadılar:

An ve masal
An ve masal

and I a goddess,
flew for days together in the twilight.

My neck frail
my heart empty
I brushed the trees with my face,
I brushed the wind with my eyes in sorrow.
The journeys I made
the nightless sky
where I flew
tired as the god
who sits in the field of clouds,
all whispered:

The moment, the legend.
The moment, the legend.

from
GOD MUST NOT SEE MY LETTERS (1999)

TÖREN GÎYSÎLERÎ

Çürümüş donuk kalbinde bu toprakların
Gözleri gördüm.
Herkes sesiyle vardı
Ve duruşuyla gövdesinin.
Bir insanı en iyi sevişirken tanırız.
Kalbimizi birlikte çürütürken.
Ağırlaşan gövdemiz
Gece uyandırır.
Mezar gibidir avlulu evler.
Çocukluk bir uykudur. Uzun sürer.
Ve dokunmak için bir arzu
Bir arzu sürükler bizi ölüme.
Ben kendimi sınadım her gövdede
Ben kendimi bıraktım her şehirde
İçime aldım göğünü ülkelerin
Ve boşluğunu görünce kalbimin
Gitmeli dedim.

Çürümüş tören giysileri içinde
Askıda salınan kökler.
Biz denize düşürsek de ateşi
O hep yanar.
Issızlık bahşeder karanlığa. Yanar.
Tarih bir yanılgı olabilir diyor şair
İnsan bir yanılgıdır diyor tanrı.
Çok sonra
Bu toprakların kalbi kadar
Çürümüş bir sonrada
İnsan bir yanılgıdır diyor tanrı.
Ve düzeltmek için varım
Ama geciktim.

Ölü kızıl suyun dalgası
Gece yürünen yol
Ve yolcuların dağıldığı zavallı yeryüzü
Salınan beyaz kefenler
Tören giysileri.

CEREMONIAL ROBES

In the cold decayed
heart of these lands
I saw eyes.
Everyone was there with their voice
and their body's pose.
We know someone best while making love,
when we corrode our hearts together.
Growing heavy, our body
wakes us in the night.
Houses with courtyards are like graves.
Childhood is a sleep, long-lasting.
And a yearning to touch,
a yearning drags us towards death.
I tested myself in every body,
I abandoned myself in every city.
I took the skies of countries to my heart
and when I saw the emptiness of my heart
I said, it's time to go.

Inside the mouldering robes of ceremony
roots sway on the hanger.
Even if we drop fire in the sea
it will burn for ever,
it burns, a gift of desolation to the dark.
Perhaps history is a mistake says the poet
mankind's a mistake says god.
Much later,
in a future corrupt as the heart of these lands,
mankind's a mistake says god,
I'm here to correct it
but too late.

The wave of red lifeless water,
the road followed at night,
the poor earth strewn with travellers,
the white swaying shrouds,
ceremonial robes.

Ve bir koşu için gerekli tek şey
Atın yelesidir.
Aslolan,
Şimdi ve burada
Çürüyüp kaldık.

Tanrı görmesin harflerimi
İnsan bir hata diyor durmadan
Ve hatasını düzeltmek için
Acı veriyor
Sadece acı.

Şubat '97, Berlin

ALLAHIN DUVARINDA BİR HARFTİR KADIN

I

Allahın duvarında bir harftir kadın
Siyah kuğuya benzer
Beklemeyi öğrenmiş

II

Ölüm
Zamana
Bekleme git dediği gün
Bildim.
Gün vurmadı yüzüne çinilerin
Çinilere yatırdım oğlumu
Boğdum.

Karnımda büyüdüğü gün bildim
Siyah bir kuğu gibi,
Allahın harflerinden süzülüp

The only thing needed for a race
is the horse's mane.
This is the truth,
now we are here
rotted away in a rut.

God must not see the letters of my script
Mankind's a mistake, he keeps saying.
And to correct his mistake
he gives sorrow,
only sorrow.

February '97 Berlin

WOMAN IS A LETTER ON ALLAH'S WALL

I

Woman is a letter on Allah's wall
She is like a black swan
She has learned to wait

II

The day
death
said to time, don't linger go,
I knew.
The sun never lit the tiles
where I laid my son
and strangled him.

The day he grew in my belly I knew
like a black swan,
gliding from Allah's letters

Avluya giren kadın
Su sesinde kendini diledi.

III

Gölgesinde şadırvanın
Günlerce bekledi.
İnsan olmak istiyordu
Kanatlarından kurtulmak.
Şadırvanda aktıkça su
Kanatları inceldi.

Ve kaldırınca kanadını
İçinde bir yılan gördü.
Değişmiş kabuğu
Zarı incelmiş.
Boynunu uzatip derine baksa
Çürümüş bir oğul görecekti

Bakmadı hiç.

IV

Avludaki dilenci
Allahın harflerini bilmeyenler
Günaha girecek diyordu şarkısında
Sela sesiyle su
Karıştı kadında

V

Ölüm zamana bekleme git derken
Bekledim avluda.
Allahın harflerini bilmiyordum
Zaman bendim
Günah da.

68

the woman entered the courtyard
she wished herself in the sound of water.

III

She waited for days
in the shadow of the fountain.
She wanted to be human
to be freed from her wings.
As water flowed in the fountain
her wings grew smaller.

And lifting her wing
She saw a snake inside.
It sloughed off its skin
its membrane was thinner.
If she stretched her neck and looked in the depths
she would see a son decayed.

She never looked.

IV

The beggar in the courtyard sang
those who don't know Allah's letters
will come to sin
in the woman has mingled
the sound of a funeral-prayer and water.

V

As death said to time, don't linger go
I waited in the courtyard.
I did not know Allah's letters
I was time
and sin.

TAŞIN İÇİNDE AVUNAN ZAMAN

I

Hasta atların
İyileşmek için dolaştığı avluda
Hasta attan da ince boynuyla
Sıska bir oğlan.
Kara uzun giysisiyle durmuş
Taş bir köprünün ortasında.
Boynunda salınan buhurdanlık
Gideceği uzaklığı gösteriyor
Ama atı hasta.
Gidemeyecek
Ay girmeyecek uykusuna.

Gitmeli
Yerini bulmalı tarih.
Söz bulmalı nesnesini.
Saçları uzamalı
Islanmalı kokuyla.

II

Taşın içinde avunan zaman
Dedi ki ona,
Gece olunca
Sürecekler sizi buradan.
Biz kalacağız.
Kartal gagası
Kar suyu
Kuyuda.
Soyunu hatırla
Tarih bitecek diyorlar
Donmuş bir fotoğrafla.

TIME CONSOLED IN THE STONE

I

In the courtyard where sick horses
circle to recover,
a puny youth
his neck thinner than the neck of a sick horse,
stands in the middle of a stone bridge
in long black clothes.
The censer swinging at his neck
shows how far he must travel,
but his horse is sick,
unable to go
and the moon shall not enter his sleep.

History must move on
and find its place.
The word must find its subject.
His hair must grow long
and be damp and fragrant.

II

Time consoled in the stone
told him,
when it's dark
you'll be driven from here.
But we will remain.
The eagle's beak
snow water
in the well.
Remember your ancestry,
they say history will end
frozen in a photograph.

İnsan yüzünü kendisi yapar
Bu yüzden rüzgâr.
Bir yer ağlayarak girer uykumuza
Ve çıkmaz.

ÇÜRÜMÜŞ KEMİKLERİN ŞARKISI

I

Ruhun bir yıldız ışığıyla parladığı gecede
Sınadım kendimi.
Kimse bilmiyor
Tepelerin küçük gizli kalplerini gördüm.
Orada gizli hayatların söylediği
Altın ve gümüşün,
Çürümüş kemiklerin şarkısı ne tuhaf.

Gece olunca herkes örtsün üstünü
O ölümcül parıltıyla
Ölümden artan o yaldızlı parıltıyla.
Uzansın herkes
Ve kadınların beyazlığından dünyayı koruyacak,
Bir toz bulunsun.
Ve göğüslerine sürülsün usulca.

Man creates his face on his own
and so there is wind.
A place weeping enters our sleep
and never leaves.

Zeytun[1] */ Maraş 1997-8*

THE SONG OF DECAYED BONES

I

At night when the soul glowed
with the light of a star
I tested myself.
Nobody knows
that I saw the little secret hearts of the hills.
How strange the song of decayed bones,
of silver and gold,
sung there by those secret lives.

As night falls let everyone cover themselves
with the deadly glitter,
the gilded glitter
left behind after death.
Let everyone swell
let there be dust
protecting the world from the whiteness of women;
let it be quietly smeared on their breasts.

[1] *Zeytun* In the south-east of Turkey, an area which once had a large Armenian population, subject to many massacres concluding with the major events of 1915.

73

II

Benim arkadaşım,
Bir kanyondaki sularda
Ardına bakmadan ilerliyor.
Ona kalsa iyi bir hayattı.
Işıklı görünüyordu yol
Ve gece uzun.
Ona kalsa herkesin bir kıyısı var.
Durup el sallayacak.

Uğurlanmak bir hayattır.
Uğurlamak da.

III

Büyünün kalbini büyüledim.
Gecenin girdim yatağına.
Kollarıma aldım ruhunu
Konuştum onunla.
Titredi;
Aslında benim zavallı varlığım
Korku neyse oydu.
Korku neyse o olacak.

MEZAR ARAYANLAR BİLİRLER

Mezar arayanlar bilirler
İçlerinde aşkla yapılmış her şey gizlidir
Savaş ve hüner
Soy ve keder.

II

In a canyon's waters
my friend wanders
and never looks back.
If you ask him, life was good,
the way well-lit and clear
and the night long.
If you ask him, we all have a shore
where we can stand and wave.

It's a life that will say farewell
and be bidden farewell.

III

I bewitched the heart of magic
and entered night's bed.
I took his soul in my arms.
I spoke to him.
he trembled;
in fact my own poor being
was fear,
what else but fear.

THOSE WHO SEARCH

Those who search for graves
know that hidden within their depths
is everything made with love
war and skill
the story of the tribe and sorrow.

Taşlı bir yolda durduk.
Fıstık ağaçlarının gölgesiz tarlasında
Antep'teydik,
Her şeyi görmüş Antep yaşlanmış
Bağrı açılmış, kanmış.
Mahçup bir çocuğun düşü gibi
Yağmur yağınca kızarır toprak.

MASAL I, II, III

MASAL I

Dilara için

I

Masalcı bir dede
Karlı bir gecede
Bir halkayla oturtur bizi
İyiyi ve kötüyü anlatırdı
Ateşi göstererek.
Ejderha'nın saltanatı boyunca
Yürütür çocukluğumuzu
Uyuturdu bahçede.

II

Benim anladığım
O soğuk
O sıcak masal gecesinde
Yüzümü döndüğüm ateş iyi,
Duvarda büyüyen gölge kötüydü.

İyilik de
Kötülük de
Bizde başlıyor
Ve bitiyordu bizde.

We stood on a stony road.
We were in Antep
in the field of pistachio trees without shade.
Antep which had seen it all, grown old,
vulnerable, sated.
The earth turns red when it rains
like a child shamed by a dream.

THREE TALES

TALE I
for Dilara

I

A grandfather teller of tales
sat us down in a ring
one snowy night.
As he showed us fire
he told us stories of good and evil.
He walked our childhood
through the dragon's empire
and lulled it to sleep in the garden.

II

That cold
that hot story-night
I understood
the fire when I turn my face was good,
the shadow looming on the wall was evil.

Good
and evil
were beginning
and ending in us.

77

MASAL II

Bir savaş tanrıçası
Ahşap, küçük köprüden geçerken,
Sandaletine yaklaşan yılan
Ona dokunmaz.

Başka yüzü yok ruhun
O ince köprü boyunca
Salınan gövdeye benzeyen yay
Tüm ormanları açar.

MASAL III

Biliyoruz ki,
Üstü açılan çocuğun yorganını
Kurt kapar.
Babaanneler bunun için var.
Yazları yer yatağında kavga
Kim kimin kardeşi
Peri kızı kimin rüyasına fısıldar.

Ama biz çocuğuz o zaman
Anahtar kimdeyse o padişah.

UZAK ÖLÜM

Marika dedesiyle su çekti kuyudan
Eski bir toprak fincana doldurdu suyu
Ve dalında sarhoş üzümlere bakarak
Güz gibi gülümsedi.
Yoksulluğu onun benzemiyor bizimkine
Ninesinin mezarına sarı güz çiçekleri koyarken.
Mum yaktı gözlerle dolu mezarlıkta
Kilise ve kuyu

TALE II

When a goddess of war
crosses the little wooden bridge
the snake sliding near her sandal
doesn't touch her.

The soul has no other face.
The bow like the body swaying
along that narrow bridge,
opens up all the forests.

TALE III

We know
the wolf grabs
the child's half-open blanket.
This is what grandmothers are for;
summer nights tussling
who is the sibling of whom,
in whose dream does the fairy queen whisper.

But we were children then,
the one with the key was king.

A DEATH FAR AWAY

Marika and her grandfather drew water from the well
Filled an old clay cup with water
And looking at the boozy grapes on the branch
Smiled like autumn.
Her poverty was not like ours
As she laid pale autumn flowers
On her grandmother's grave.
She lit a candle in the graveyard full of eyes
Church and well

Ölüm hiç bu kadar olmadı dünyada
Hiçbir yerde orada olduğu kadar.

Kasım '97, Bükreş

ADA, BEN VE DEFNE

I

Gittim ülkesine kardeşlerimin
Dağılmış bir rahmin suyuyla örtünmüş,
Güneşe serilmiş kalpleri kurumuş.

II

Gittim ülkesine kardeşlerimin
İçimde koyu bir aşk isteği.
Gövdem dağılmak istiyor,
Karışmak istiyor topraklarına.
Oysa yok toprakları
Her yer taş.
Ve orada, öyle ağır ki tarih.
Taşların arasında
Gözlerinin sırrıyla
Hayatı arıyorlar.

Buğulu bir sabahta
Yaratılan deniz
Söyledi bana "tüm o masallar bizimdi"
Bizimdi o kesik gövdeler.
Ve bir gizdi yaratılan.
Şimdi bu taşların eksik ruhuyla,
Bu gözlerin, göğüslerin,
Yapmaya yetmediği insanlığımızla
Bizimdi o geçmiş.

There was never such a death in the world
Nowhere like that one.

November 1997 Bucharest

THE ISLAND, MYSELF AND THE LAUREL

I

I went to the land of my kin
veiled in the waters of a scattered womb,
spread under the sun to dry, their hearts withered.

II

I went to the land of my kin
within me a deep love-longing.
My body wants to break up,
to mix with their earth.
But they have no earth
only rock.
And a dense history.
With their eyes' mystery
they search for life
among the stones.

The sea
created one misty morning,
told me, "all those tales were ours".
Ours were those severed bodies
and creation a secret.
With our humanity that all these eyes and breasts,
and all these soulless stones
were not enough to make,
that past was ours.

81

III

Taşların arasında
Mutsuz, kara bakışlı adamlar
Bakınıyordu.
Kesik gövdelerle doluydu ülkeleri.
Kesik başlar ve görmeyen gözlerle.
Bir sırrın parçasıydı her şey.
Birleşmeyecek onca gövde,
Onca kol
Dağılmış beklemekte.
Bu mu diyorlar zamanı kanıtlar,
Bu kesik gövdelerin acısızlığı?

Zamanı kanıtlamak için
Doruklara kaleler kurmalı.

Sözcüklerden başka yeri olmayan
O kavim,
Uyumuş sözün huzursuz yatağında.
Ve o uykudan,
Uyanmamış.

IV

Defne ağacını alıp karşıma
Dedim ki ona "Kardeşlerimin ülkesinde sen,
Bir müjdesin hâlâ. Hayatı hatırlatıyorsun onlara.
Eskiyi bilen ağaçların soyundan
Ve ruhu sarhoş kokuyla."

Yola çıktım
Yolun anneyi unutturan oğullara
Ağırlığı.
Ülkesini yitiren kaptan,
Sulara ruh fısıldayan.

III

Unhappy glowering men
were peering
among the stones.
Their land was full of broken bodies,
severed heads, unseeing eyes,
everything part of a mystery.
All those bodies will never come together,
all those scattered limbs
keep waiting.
Is this proof of time, they ask,
that these broken bodies feel no pain?

Surely proofs of time
must be the forts erected on the hilltops.

That tribe
with nowhere to be but in words,
fell asleep in the restless word-bed
and never woke up
from that sleep.

IV

I addressed the laurel tree before me.
"In the land of my kin
you are still the sacred gift
which reminds them of life.
You're from the race of trees
that knows the past,
its soul drunk with the smell."

I set out on the way,
a way so hard
it makes sons forget their mothers.
The skipper losing sight of his land
whispers soul into the waters.

Bir defne yaprağı,
Kesik bir baş
Bir mum ölülere yol olan.
Bir mum,
Kızıl ve ağır kokan.

V

Koca bir orman gölgesi ve sesleri tanrıların,
Kimse kalmadı burada sudan.
İstek bir bıçak gibi girer gözlerine
Ve çıkmaz.

VI

Dili varsa kuyunun
Söyleyecektir,
Derinlik kendine bakmasındadır insanın,
Gözlerini içine daldırmasında.
Ve nem,
Sesi alıp ağırlaştıran,
Dipleri dolaştırıp yoran nem.
Kim söylerse söylesin şarkıyı
Çoban kadınların sesine benzetir.

VII

Kesik başını tanrımın,
Kovdum evimden.
Ve alıp karşıma gövdesini
Dedim ki ona,
Bu taşların arasında yatan zaman
Bir şey değil aslında.
Mutsuzluğumuz o bizim
Ve kalbimizi çıkarıp
Güneşte kanatacak kadar
Geniş göğümüz
Ve ruhumuz kara.

A laurel leaf,
a severed head,
a candle that leads to the dead,
a candle
flaming and heavy-scented.

V

Shadow of a great forest, the voices of gods,
no one left here from the sea.
Desire pierces their eyes like a knife
and never leaves.

VI

If the well had a tongue
it would say
that depth is a person searching the self,
the gaze plunged within.
And moisture
makes its voice heavy
and winds round the depths.
Whoever sings the song
will think it's the voice of shepherd women.

VII

I chased the severed head of my god
from my house.
I addressed him straight and said,
Actually, time that lies among these stones
means nothing.
It is our unhappiness.
Our sky is so spacious
that we can remove our hearts
and make them bleed in the sun,
Our soul is dark.

VIII

Denizle oyun oynadık biz.
Biriktiren ve ayıran
Tutan ve yıkan.
Geçmiş için gidilen yol,
Şaşırmak içindi.
Bulduğumuzu sandığımız her şey çocukluk.
Serin avlu
Ve sokak başlarında
Birer hırsız gibi bekleyen kuyular.
Kalbi göğün içinde
Ve kapağını kaldırsan
Sana göğü verir.
Sessizliğine katar seni

Boğuntusuna.

IX

Mutlu olamadık hiç.
Nasıl da kederle bakınıyoruz sonraya.
Sınır ve sınırsızlık kavşağı belki.
Belki de, bir rahmin zemininde,
Dünyaya bakmak bilgisi.
Ruhun çaresizliğini anlayan ışık
Kör etti bizi.

Tarihi gördük sadece, hayatı değil.
Kesik gövdelerden yoruldu zihnimiz
Ve şefkati hatırlatacak kadın yok.
Yıkanan bir kadının yumuşaklığını,
Avluya saklayıp,
Yanı başına bir kuyu kazmakla,
Kaderimizi yeniledik.

VIII

We played games with the sea,
it divides and gathers together,
sustaining, destroying.
The road we took back to the past
was bewilderment.
Everything we thought we found was childhood.
A cool courtyard
and at the head of every street a well
each lurking like a thief.
The sky's heart within,
and if you raise the lid
it gives you the sky
and adds you to its silence

and suffocates.

IX

We could never be happy.
We look at the future, it bewilders us.
Perhaps there's some crossroad
of boundary and no boundary.
And perhaps on the floor of a womb
is the knowledge to read the world.
The light knowing the soul is helpless
has made us blind.

We saw only history, not life,
our minds exhausted by broken bodies,
and never a woman to remind us of tenderness.
But in the courtyard was hidden
the softness of a woman bathing,
digging a well beside her
we renewed our fate.

X

Aşk kadar eskidir hayat.
Taşlar aşk kadar sert.
Büyü nemle girer uykumuza
Ve çıkmaz.
Bir çığlık anı içime aldığım ölüm,
Doğurduğum ve dünyaya saldığım,
Ruhum n'olur gir uykuma
Ruhum n'olur rüyada acı olan
Hayat için, bana fısılda.

XI

Tek gözüyle ahtapotun
Kapandım içime.
Acıma uyandıran ten
Ve ülke.

XII

Gittim ülkesine kardeşlerimin
Yoksul ve umutsuzdular.
Gövdemle durdum güvertede
Sınır ve sınırsızlık algım
Orada sınandı.
Bende başlayan ve bende biten
Her şeyi gördüm.
O ülkenin dağınık gövdesi kadar
Dağınıktım.

Temmuz '97, Rodos-Symi

88

X

Life is as old as love,
stones hard as love.
Magic will bedew our sleep
and never leave.
I welcome death, a moment's scream;
and soul, whom I bore and sent into the world,
come, enter my sleep,
come, my soul, bitter in dream,
for the sake of life
whisper to me.

XI

I closed in on myself
with the single eye of an octopus.
My body, my land
woke me to pain.

XII

I went to the land of my kin,
they were poor, without hope.
My body and I stood on the deck.
My perception of boundaries
was tested there.
I saw all
beginning and ending in me.
I was as scattered
as the broken body of that land.

July '97, Rhodes-Symi

PENCEREDEKİ TANRI

I

Beyaz gözlü tanrımı
Boynundan öpen salyangoz
Emdi kanını.
Ve tanrım yalnızlaştı.
Tanrım biliyor,
Böyle öpülmek aşkla olur
Ve aşk öldürür.

II

Beyaz gözleriyle
Bakıyor tanrım pencereden.
Ölü beyaz gözleriyle.
Soruyor "ne yapıyorsun"
Ben yüzümü saklarsam tanrıdan
Yazık ederim.
Yüzüm onundur
Onun ince ellerinin

III

Penceremden bana bakan kesik başlı tanrı
Kirlendikçe yapıyor yüzünü
Kirlendikçe öğreniyor bakmayı.

AYAK İZLERİ

Bir kuyuya eğildiğinde
Yüzünü görecek su yoksa
Çekil.
Öldürse de su seni

THE GOD AT THE WINDOW

I

The snail that kisses
my blank-eyed god on his neck
has sucked his blood.
And my god's become lonely.
My god knows
to be kissed like this means love
and love kills.

II

My god looks through the window
with his blank eyes,
his dead white eyes.
"What are you doing?" he asks.
It's pointless
to hide my face from the god.
My face belongs to him
and his fine hands.

III

The god with the severed head
who looks at me through my window,
gathering dirt creates his face.
Gathering dirt he learns to look.

FOOTPRINTS

When you bend over a well
when there's no water
to see your face
draw back.

Görerek öldürür
Susuz kuyudan kork

Kuru düşünme cehennemi
Nemlidir
Ve ayak izleri vardır.
Önceden
Gidecek olan herkesin.

YERYÜZÜNÜN DÜŞÜ

Göğün gecesi yalnızken
Düşünmüş,
Bu yıldızlar niçin?
Neden içimin karanlığında uğuldayan bu ses?
Sesler çekilse
Ne kalır
Ruhumu kemiren boğuntudan geriye?

Kutup yıldızı yerinden oynasa bir an,
Balıkçı mı şaşırır yolunu,
Çoban mı unutur ıslığını?
Belki de hiçbir şey,
Hiçbir şey hakikatimi değiştirmez.
Yeryüzünün düşüyüm ben
Uykusunu bitiren insan
Uyanınca görecek
Asıl karanlık ötede.

Even though water kills you
it kills you on sight.
Beware the waterless well.

The dry hell of thought
is moist.
And there are footprints
of all who go before.

EARTH'S DREAM

In its loneliness the night sky
thought,
Why these stars?
Why this voice humming in my heart of darkness?
When the voices recede
what's left
but oppression gnawing at my soul?

If the Pole Star moves one second from its place,
does the fisherman lose his way?
Does the shepherd forget his whistle?
Perhaps nothing,
nothing, can alter the truth of me.
I am earth's dream.
A sleeper ending his sleep
will see when he wakes,
real darkness beyond.

DÜNYADA OLMAK ACIDIR. ÖĞRENDİM.

Yeryüzündeki tüm kızıl taşlara
Tanrının kanı sürülmüştür.
Bu yüzden kızıl taşlar
Çocukluğumuzu öğretir.
Tanrı, biz çocukken,
Yanımızda dolaşır.
Küpemize dokunur
Ve kolyemize.
Pabuçlarımıza ve kurdelamızın
Kızçocuk olmak kıvrımına girer
Saklanır.

Kızıl bir elbise ve yatak almalıyım,
Kızıl bir yüzük,
Ve lamba.
O zaman olmalı ki,
Annenin zamanı başlar ve tükenir.

Beklemeyi bilen kan,
Taş olmayı da bilir.
Dünyada olmak acıdır. Öğrendim.

Kızıl karanlık
Mavi karanlık
Ve başlangıç
Bir anlamı olmalı ki bunların,
Bırakmaz bizi annemiz ve tanrımız.

TO BE IN THE WORLD IS PAIN.

All the red stones on earth are smeared
with blood of the god.
And that's why red stones
teach our childhood.
When we are children, the god
walks beside us.
He touches our ear-rings
and necklace.
He enters and hides in our shiny shoes
and the folds of our childish ribbon.

I must buy a flame-red dress and bed,
a red ring
and lamp.
There must come a time
when the mother's time begins and ends.

The blood that knows how to wait,
also knows how to be a stone.
To be in the world is pain –
this I have learned.

Red darkness
blue darkness
and the beginning,
the meaning of these must be
that they never abandon us,
our mother and our god.

from
SONS REARED BY THE MOON (2002)

AYNI TOPRAKLARDA

Güneş solumda ve dikenlerin yolunu aydınlatıyor.
Çocukluğumla aramda ölüm var.
Ölümle hayat arasına sıkışmış, uykulu, kadim bir tepedeyim.
Annem yoldan gelmiş yol olmuş kardeşime,
Ölümleri gösteriyor. Birlikte ağlıyorlar.
Ben güneşe ağlayacağım. Issızlığına bu tepelerin.
Ve yanımda, soyunmuş derisiyle bir yılanın, çok istese
Lapis olacak mavi bir taşın rehavetiyle bakınıyorum.
Neresi yurdum?
Güneş belki de.
O hep duran. Çocukluğumu tanıyan eski dostum kaplumbağa.
Mezarları hatırlatarak, küçük bir kızın yanağından öper ve
Hoşça kal der. Dön annene.
Git ve unut yaradılışı.
Güneşe bakarak kanını akıtmış arkadaşını
Ve yılanların hikâyelerini unutmalısın.
Gözaltlarına yerleşen çizgiler
Çocukluğa dönüyorsa,
Aynı topraklarda,
Gelinciklere bakınca,
Aşk başlar.

BABA OCAĞINA DÖNEN

Baba ocağına dönen karanlığa dönecek.
Sadece orada büyümek olan kan.
Ev içlerinde...

Her şey hatırlanacak.

IN THE SAME LANDS

The sun on my left lights up the path of thorns.
Between me and my childhood is death.
I'm on an ancient hilltop, sleepy, stuck between life and death.
My mother shows the dead
to my brother who made the journey
and has become the journey.
They weep together.
I will weep to the sun, to the desolation of these hills.
Beside me a snake stripped of his skin,
I look about with the languor of a blue stone
which can become lapis lazuli if it desires.
Where is my land?
The sun, perhaps.
Always there, my old friend the tortoise
who knows my childhood,
kisses a little girl's cheek and warns her of graves.
Farewell, he says, go back to your mother.
Go and forget creation.
You must forget snake-stories and your friend
who shed his blood looking at the sun.
When lines settle under your eyes
love begins,
returning to childhood
looking at poppies
in the same lands.

THE RETURN

The return to the paternal hearth
will be a return to darkness.
Only there does blood grow.
In the very heart of the home…

Everything will be remembered.

ÇÜRÜME, TANRIDAN GİZLENEN

Keskin bir kılıçla toprağa çizilmiş
Dar ve kavuşmasız sokaklar.
Kan izi, kaçıyor hayat.
Küf, eski yurdun belleğinden akarak,
Giriyor duvarlara.

Çürüme, tanrıdan gizlenen.
Ve kurban edilecek oğul hazır.

Kediler, eski karanlık prenslerin yerinde,
Uzun kuyruklarıyla duruyorlar.
Fıskiyelerin gölgesi,
Dişli hançer,
İçerde ilerleyen çelik.
Ve bir halktan artakalan lehçe,
Tütsü,
Merdiven.

Her kapı eğilecek bir boynu bekliyor.

SUSKUN EV

Avlusunda beklemek olan suskun ev,
Ölüm sandı geceyi. Ve dünyadan ayrıldı.

DECAY, HIDDEN FROM GOD

Streets etched on the earth with a sharp sword,
narrow, no meeting points.
Traces of blood, life leaking away.
Pouring from the memory of an ancient land,
mould enters the walls.

Decay hidden from god.
And the son to be sacrificed, ready.

Instead of the old princes of darkness,
cats remain with their long tails.
The shadow of fountains,
the serrated dagger,
the steel that probes within.
And the dialect surviving from a people,
incense,
the staircase.

Every door waits for a neck
to be bowed in submission.

SILENT HOUSE

The silent house was waiting in its courtyard.
It thought night was death. And parted from the world.

ÇOCUK MEZARLARI

Öldük işte.
Kaydık karanlıktan.
Kayın ağaçları da gördü,
Ufak taşlar da.

Gece ve yıldızlar geçti üzerimizden.
Gömüldük yol kıyısına.

ŞAHMARAN

O büyük dağın eteğinde
Bir Şahmaran oturuyor.
O büyük dağın eteğinde ölüm,
Doymuyor.

YALNIZLIK

Yalnızlık
Yırtılmış sesinde bir çobanın
Dağlarda yakalar insanı.

CHILDREN'S GRAVES

So we died.
We slipped away out of darkness.
Beech trees saw us
and tiny stones.

Night and stars passed over us.
We were buried by the roadside.

SHAHMARAN

At the foot of the great mountain
a basilisk lives.
At the foot of the great mountain death,
insatiable.

LONELINESS

The loneliness
in the ragged voice of a shepherd
grips us in the mountains.

TANRIYLA KONUŞMA

Allah'ı gördüm. İçi oyulmuş bir haznede bekliyordu.
Ruhunun karanlığına girdim oturdum.

I

Bir dağ gölünde uyandı Allah.
Bakındı ve mahmur başını çevirdi.
Ne güzeldi dünya.
Döndü uykusuna. Kalbi dayanmayacak.
Kalpsiz. Ve biz ondan artakalan lavlar
Örseliyoruz dalgayı.
Gölü huzursuz bir taşla karıştırıp,
Dolduruyoruz acımızla.

II

Bir dağ gölünde uyandı Allah
"gidin" dedi. "soyunuzu çekin toprağımdan"
Onu gördüm. Çook beklemiş bir bakışla baktı bana.
Evler gizledi ölüleri. Kıpırdadı ağaçlar.

III

Huzursuz . . .
Yaratıcı değil ve henüz yok yeryüzü.
O göl uykusundan uyanıp
Gözlerini uzatsa,
Bir buzul kayacak dünyanın karanlığına.

Ve insan orada bekliyor olmayacak.

I saw Allah. He was waiting in a hollowed-out tank.
I entered the darkness of his soul and sat down.

I

Allah woke up in a mountain lake.
He turned his languid head and looked around.
How beautiful the world!
He went back to sleep. His heart can't stand it.
Heartless. And we his left-over lava,
ruffle the wave.
Stirring the lake with a troubled stone
we fill it with our sorrow.

II

Allah woke up in a mountain lake.
"Go" he said. "Remove your people from my land."
I saw him. He looked at me with a long expectant look.
Houses hid the dead. Trees moved.

III

Troubled…
Not creative and still there is no earth.
When he wakens from that sleep in the lake
and opens his eyes wide,
a glacier will slide into the world's darkness.

And no human will be waiting there.

SÖZCÜKLER ACIMIZI DOLDURMAYACAK

Siyah örtüyle kapatılmış, ölüme hazırlanan bir gelin gibi duran masada, konuştum onlarla. Yanımızdan bir şair hırsız gibi geçti. Sözün uçurduğu gövdesiyle. Şairlere baktım. Hepsi bir gölgeyi dolaştırıyor. Bir köpeği dolaştırır gibi.

Sözcükler acımızı doldurmayacak.

Casablanca / temmuz / 2001

WORDS

I talked with them at a table
shrouded in black, a bride adorned for death.
A poet passed us like a thief. His body a flight of stolen words.
I looked at the poets. Each walking a shadow
like taking a dog for a walk.

Words will never fill up our pain.

Casablanca / July 2001

from
IN HIS DESERT (2002)

BUZUL

O gölde buzlarla çevrilmiş, binlerce yıldır ölüydüm.
Uyandırdın.
Uyandım ve yanmış bir ormanın sisinde buldum uykumu.
Geceye yapıştı gövdem.

Bir buzulun derin ışığından tene akan beyazlık
Hatırlattı;

O gölde yürüdün sen.
Ten ve iz bırakarak.

YARADILIŞ

Dinle bak, dağlar oluşuyor.
Yer altı nehirleri çekiliyor
İçinin pıhtılaşmış kanına.
Lapis bir damar
Toz zerreleri.
Belki bir rüzgâr tanıyor yeryüzünü.

Ağaçlara ve insana dokunup ölüyor rüzgâr.

HER KADIN KENDİ AĞACINI TANIR

Sana geldiğimde
Kanatlarımı,
Siyah taşlarla örülmüş
O ıssız şehrin üzerinde açacak,
Bulduğum bir ağacın dallarına tüneyecek
Ve acıyla bağıracaktım.

110

THE GLACIER

For thousands of years I lay dead, turned to ice in that lake.
You woke me.
I woke and found my sleep in the mist of a forest blighted with fire.
My body clung to night.

Whiteness flowed into my skin from a glacier's deep light
and reminded me

You walked in that lake
leaving tracks and skin.

CREATION

Listen and look, mountains rise into being.
Underground rivers shrink
to sluggish inner blood.
A lapis-blue vein
atoms of dust.
Perhaps only a wind knows earth.

The wind touches trees and humans and dies away.

EVERY WOMAN KNOWS HER OWN TREE

When I came to you
I was going to open my wings
over that deserted city
built of black stones,
and find a tree and perch on its branches
and shout with pain.

111

Her kadın kendi ağacını tanır.

Uçtum o gece.
Karanlığın girmeye korktuğu şehri geçtim.
Gölge olmayınca ruh yalnızdı. Uludum.

KARA BİR YAĞMUR

Ört üstümü.
Kabuk değiştireyim.
Gün gibi, kuşları gibi sabahın.
Kara bir yağmur yağarken.

SABIR TANRISININ TAPINAĞINDA KONAKLAMA

I

Yağmurlu dağların arasından gurbetini seçtin.

Son gece beklediğin yer
Sabır tanrısının eviydi.
İnsanı merhametle donatmanın evi.
Tapınaklara gerek yok dedim.
Burası sadece bir yer.
İnsanın ruhu tapınak kılınmalı.
Ve yağmur, yersizliğin nehri.
Tanrıdan ve çocukluktan hatırlanan.

Every woman knows her own tree.

That night I flew.
I passed over the city that darkness feared to enter.
Having no shadow the soul
was lonely.

I howled like a dog.

BLACK RAIN

Cover me up.
Let me change my shell,
like day, like birds of the morning.
While a black rain falls.

NIGHT SPENT IN THE TEMPLE OF A PATIENT GOD

I

You chose your exile among rainswept mountains.

Where you lingered last night
was the home of the patient god
the home where a human is equipped with compassion.
No need for temples, I said.
This is simply a place.
The human soul must surely be a temple.
And rain the river of homelessness
reminds us of god and childhood.

II

Yağmurlu dağların arasından gurbetini seçtin.

Yanılmanın güzelliği
Ve huzuru acının.
Her şey seni bir boşluğa uladı.
Ve sen, sarı sabır çiçeklerine bakıp ağladın.
Onun koynunda yokmuş gibi uyudun.
Bir dağa gidilecek, gurbet seçilecek.
Ve insan istenecek tanrıdan.

Tekrar dinlemeli o müziği.
Sevişmenin tamamlanmadığı o yer.

UYKUSU KAÇTI DÜNYANIN

Bana, usulca eğildiğim vadide ağlamamı söyledi.
Ağlarsam unutacak, gölgelerle oynamayacaktım.
Bana, usulca yaban bir böğürtlenin dikenine dokun ama geç yanından,
Durma dedi.
Bekledim.
İçinde su olmayan mermer kaba eğildim.
Ona duvardaki gözlerin taştan olup olmadığını sordum.
Beni bırak dedim.
Göle gitsek.
Taşlar ayaklarımızı kesse. Yüzsek.

Yıldızlardan beklediğin verildi sana sonunda.
Artık aşksız ve beklentisizsin.
Gir göle. Duvarda incelen ışığa bak. Günahı öğren.
Unut sonra.

Böğürtlen aramalıyız ormanda.
Gün doğuyor. Uykusu kaçtı dünyanın.

Lodeve / temmuz / 2000

II

You chose your exile among rainswept mountains.

The beauty of making mistakes
and the peace of pain.
Everything led you to emptiness.
And you, you looked at the pale flowers of patience and wept
You slept in his arms as though nothing existed.
There shall be a journey made to the mountain and exile chosen
And a human required of god.

We must listen again to that music.
That place was not meant for loving.

THE SLEEP OF THE WORLD HAS FLED

He told me to weep, in the valley where I bent in silence
If I wept I would forget, I would not dance with shadows
Gently touch a wild blackberry thorn but pass by,
don't stay, he told me.
I waited.
I leaned over the marble vessel empty of water.
I asked if the eyes on the wall were of stone or not.
Leave me, I said.
We should go to the lake,
if the stones cut our feet, we should swim.

At last you were granted your hopes from the stars.
But from now on you're without love or hope.
Enter the lake. Look at the dwindling light on the wall. Learn about sin.
Then forget.

We must search for the blackberry in the forest.
Sunrise. The sleep of the world has fled.

Lodeve / July / 2000

AŞK KUYUSU

Duvarında el ve yürek izi olan aşkın
Kuyusuna düştün.

YALNIZLIK

Taşlar için de yalnızlık gerekli.
Zeytin ağaçları
Ve koyu gölgelerin gizlendiği ev içleri için de.

ORMANIN TAA İÇİNDEN

Deniz Bilgin'in tamamlayamadığı son resmine verdiği ad "Ormanın
Taa İçinden "di. Biraz da Deniz'e anlatılmadığı için eksik kalan bir aşktan.

Bir yabanın gözleri ve adımlarıyla
Yaklaştım ormana.
Onunla bir ağacın altında uyuyup
Yeniden doğacaktım.
Ormana karışmanın acısı ve ışığıyla.

Bu onun izi.
Ormanda sürülen
Ve bir ağaca bakarak insanı iyileştiren hayat gibi.

Şimdi, ilk kez yaratılan bir denizin öfkesiz anında
Işıkların göğü bölme isteğine takılıyor aklım.
Onun çocukluğuna.

THE WELL OF LOVE

You fell into the well of love
which had traces of hand and heart
on its wall.

LONELINESS

Stones too need loneliness.
And olive trees
and the inside of houses where dark shadows lurk.

FROM DEEP IN THE FOREST

*In memory of Deniz Bilgi who named her last unfinished picture "From
Deep in the Forest". And partly too because of an unhappy love affair
never confided to Deniz.*

I approached the forest
with the eyes and steps of a savage.
I would sleep by him under a tree
and be reborn,
in pain and light becoming part of the forest.

Here are his tracks
like life that heals
when we're exiled to the forest and look at a tree.

Now, at the moment of calm when a sea is first created
my mind clings to its childhood
and the wish to separate sky from light.

Deniz kıpırdıyor. Aşk bu. Anne isteği gövdenin.

Dağlara dönüyorum. Vurulacak geyikler su içmeye indiğinde
Nasıl bakacaklar dünyaya.
Ve o silahını tetiklediğinde
Nasıl çırpınacak gövde.

Denizden çıkmaya uğraşan yengecin acemi elleri.
Onun acımadığı eller.

Şimdi güz uyandırmalı aklımı
Ve aşk sandığımı kapatmalı.

Tavana yakın odada uyurken
Tavana bakıp ağlamıştım.
Uyuyor sanıyordum dünyayı.
Her şeyi uyuyor sanıyordum
Avutmuştu bu beni.

Gece yaktığı muma biriken kanatlardan duyduğum ses
"ormanın taa içi sensin. oraya vardığında kimse olmayacak.
Sadece sessizlik ve hakkı verilmiş hayat" diyordu.
Ürperdim... döndüm uyuyordu.

Nişan alınmış her şey sonsuzlukta kesilmiş ve gelecekte
bir yaralıdır.

Sessizlik aşkta sınandı ve bir uyku odasında bekletildi.
Gündoğumu dünyaya fısıldanacak bir müjdeyle yayıldı ve
Uyandırdı ormanı. İnsanın ümidi gizlendi ormana.
Ve dendi ki,
İnsan dünyaya sırtını döndüğünde, sığınacağı tek yer orman olacak.
Ağaçların gördüğünü görebilseydi eğer.

Beni her sabah bir ağacın altında buluyordu.
Ağacı uyandırarak önce.

The sea stirs. It's love. The body's desire for the mother.

I return to the mountains. When deer doomed to be shot
go down to the water to drink
how they will look at the world.
When the trigger is pulled
how the body will quiver.

The crab's clumsy claws struggling out of the sea.
Hands without pity.

Now autumn must waken my mind
and seal my love-chest.

Sleeping in the attic
I looked at the ceiling and wept.
Thinking the world was asleep
thinking everything was asleep
consoled me.

At night I heard a voice from wings touching the candle-flame,
"The deep heart of the forest is you; when you reach it, no one
will be there.
Only silence and the claims of life," it said.
I shivered – and turned, he was sleeping.

Everything aimed at
is a wound in the future
and comes to an end in infinity.

Silence was tested in love, kept waiting in a room of sleep.
Dawn was announced to the world in joyful whispers,
and awoke the forest. Human hope hid in the forest.
And they said:
For the one who turns his back on the world
the only shelter is the forest.
If only he could have seen what the trees saw.

Every morning first wakening the tree
he found me under that tree.

Bıçağı çeken inancı tazeleyecek.
Önce kim koklayacak kını.
Sedef ve meşin.
Rüyamda avını anlatıyordu.
Bir ormanda anlatıyordu avını.
Bıçakları ve giysileri vardı.
Öldürmeyi değil
İzlemeyi anlattı.
Beklemeyi.

Omzuna uzandım.
Yaz geçiyor ve bana bir resim kalıyor ondan:
Bir ormanda kaybolma isteğisin sen.
Yanlış yerde ümitlenmenin, bir yalanla büyümenin intikamı sanki.
Hayatın deli bir gömlekle başıma geçirdiği aşk.
Koştum ve yitirdim tanrımı.
"Tanrı gelişir" Kendini tanrı gören herkesin bedeninde büyür.
Köş ormanında. Ağaçlara bak ağla. Yağmur yağıyor
Ve kalbimi sıkıştıran el...

Onun içinde gürültü var.
Bense sessizliği yemişim sanki.
İçimde uyuyor sessizlik uyanıyor.

Benim için de bir ağaç büyüt.

İlk gece bir uğultuyla uyandım.
Ağaçlara tüneyen kuşların
Kanat seslerini dinletti bana.
Koynumda uyu dedi.
Korkma.
Duyduğum sadece kanat sesiydi.
Dalları yararak yerini yapan,
Onun ıslığına gelen kuşlar.
Mavi pencere, kötülük.
Kaçırılmış bir hayat varmış gibi geride

Whoever draws the knife
will renew his belief.
Who will first smell the sheath?
Leather and mother-of-pearl.
He was describing the hunt in my dream.
He was describing the hunt in a forest.
He had knives and hunting garments.
Not to kill, he explained
but to track
and wait.

I leant on his shoulder.
Summer passes and I have a picture of him:
you are a wish to be lost in a forest,
revenge for growing up with a lie,
for hopes unfulfilled.
Life hit me over the head
with love in a crazy shirt.
I ran and lost my god.
"God develops". In everyone's body grows one
who sees himself as god.
Run in your forest. Look at the trees and weep. Rain falls
and a hand is squeezing my heart...

There is tumult within him.
As though I had consumed silence.
Silence sleeps in me and wakens.

For me too grow a tree.

The first night I woke to an uproar.
He made me listen to the wingbeats of birds perching in the trees.
Sleep on my breast, he said.
Don't be afraid.
It was only the sound of bird-wings.
Birds come to his whistle,
splitting the branches to find a perch.
The blue window means danger.
I remembered the wind back then

Rüzgârı hatırladım.
Ve korktum kuyudan.
Ormana gidelim dedim.
Ağaçlara bakıp ağlayalım.
Belki uzanır bir ağacın altında yeniden doğarız.

Ve doğdum ben.
Beni doğurdu o ormanda...
Bıraktı.

Ruha değmiş ondurulmuş istek.
Tenim inceldi ve öyle açık ki acıya.
Gördüm kanatlarını bana doğru uçan kötülüğün.
Katı ve dilsiz olduğu doğanın yalan.
Beni bir ağaca yaslayıp yüzümü tuttuğunda
Aşk ondan fazlaydı.

Bir ağacın yanından ona benzeyerek geçtim.

Dağlara yayılan
Vadilere tutunan ağaçların
İnadından söz etti bana.

Dağdan alınan dağa döndüğünde
Onun olmayacak.

Taa içine gözbebeklerinin yürüdüm. Ağaçların sessiz ülkesinde.
Yabanların sürülmüş izlerine basarak.
Avucumda bir gül yaprağını ezerek baktım kuyuya.
Ve kokusunu duydum tutulmanın.
Karanlık uğursuz bir yılan zehrini akıtmak için dönerken yatağında
"dinle" dedim "bu sesler bin yıldır var. bu orman, bu deniz.
Arzun iyiliğe
dönüştüğünde
sen de..."

Dünya bir kalbe sığınarak okşanmayı bekledi.

Tüketilmiş, karanlığa bırakılmış akıl.
Bir sancının yılan parıltısında süren yayılması.

122

like a life I escaped from.
And I was afraid of the well.
"Let's go to the forest", I said,
"let's look at the trees and weep.
Perhaps we can lie beneath a tree and be reborn."

And I was born.
He gave me birth in the forest…
and left me.

Desire touched my soul and was healed,
my body shrank and opened to pain.
I saw the wings of evil flying towards me.
It's a lie that nature is dumb and violent.
When he leant me against a tree and held my face
love was greater than he.

In the likeness of a tree, I approached a tree.

It told me of the stubbornness of trees
that cling to valleys
and spread to mountains.

What is taken from the mountain and returns to the mountain
will not be his.

I walked deep among your darlings. In the silent land of trees,
treading in the smeared tracks of savages.
Squeezing a rose-petal in my palm I looked down the well
and felt the smell of the love-bolt.
The evil ill-omened snake returning to shed its poison in your bed.
"Listen," I said, "these sounds have been here for a thousand years,
this forest, this sea,
you and your wish to be transformed
to goodness…"

The world sheltered in a heart and waited to be caressed.

But the exhausted mind was abandoned to darkness.
The spreading of pain that keeps unfolding in a snake's glitter.

Tanrı seçti bizi,
Kendi yalnızlığını duyurmak için,
Aşkı verdi

Gece ormanın karanlık yüzüyle baktı bana.
Puhu kuşu anladı.
Ve gagasını kendi kalbine batırdı.
Hırıltılarla anlatmak istedi.
Kimse yok... Kimse yok... durma.

Bir ağacın çıplaklığıyla yaklaşıyorum kışa.

Bir gölde uyandırdı beni.
Sol omzumdan öperek
Güneşi gösterdi.
Damlanın nilüferle yüzdüğü
Dağ sabahı.
Her şey yenilendi.
Kalp aldanır. Ahmaktır.
Ve ben incindim.
Rüzgâr dalları kımıldatıyor
Deliliği, ölme isteğini.

Göle yansıyan yaprakları sarartan gövde biliyor.
Düşmeyi bekliyorum.
Boynumdan öpülecek ve bırakılacağım kış ormanına.

Aşk ağaçlardan ağıyor.
Damarların ince telaşı, inadı bende yok.
Çok gidemem yanlış toprak.

Varolma isteği doğanın.
Taşlar, kır çiçekleri.
Aldırışsız görünüp birbirlerine
Nasıl da gözetiyorlar.

Ben her şeyi bırakıyorum.
Aşkı
Bir yası taşımayı.

The god chose us,
and gave us love
so we might feel his loneliness.

At night he looked at me with the dark face of the forest.
The eagle-owl understood
and sank his beak in his own heart.
He wanted his screeches to explain.
No one there... No one there... don't stay.

Like a bare tree I'm near to winter.

He woke me in a lake
And kissing my left shoulder
showed me the sun.
Mountain morning
droplets swimming with water-lilies.
Everything was renewed.
The heart can be deceived. A fool.
And I was hurt.
Wind stirs the branches,
madness, the death-wish.

The trunk sees in the lake-mirror
its leaves turning yellow.
I am waiting to fall.
A kiss on my neck, I'll be left in the winter forest.

Love rises from the trees.
In me there is no fine flutter of veins,
no stubbornness.
In the wrong land I don't go far.

Nature's need to exist.
Stones, wild flowers,
they seem to ignore
but how much they watch over each other.

I leave everything
love
and mourning.

Kar yağacak
Ve omzumdaki siyah şal
Arkadaşımın ölümü olacak.

Deniz çekildiğinde rüya başlar.
o rüyada büyük bir bahçe.
o bahçede uyku kokan toprak.
gözlerimi dikeceğim ormana.
ve kanımda ilerleyen sabır
bitecek sonunda.

Gece gördü her şeyi.
Gövdeden eksilen kanı,
İncelmesini belin.
Aya söylenecek ne varsa söylendi.
Beni içimde bir bıçakla bıraktı.
Yapraklara bakıyorum,
Ağzımdaki acı tadın bozduğu ruhuma.
Derin ve karanlık bir istek belki de suların fısıldadığı

Kalbin koyu taşlarına bas, geç kıyıdan.

İnsanlar hayatımıza girer ve usulca çıkarlar.
Bir yer kayması,
Belki de bir ağacın dallarının uzamasından farksız.

Karacalar vurulduğunda çırpınan gövde
Yaşama isteğidir güzelliğin.

Karanlık bizden sonra olacakları taşır, sezdirir bize.

zümrüd-ü anka falda görünse
yeniden doğmaya işaret. keşke.
yeniden doğmayacak.
kış ve karanlık bir istek.
kar yağıyor, bir parsın kemikleri
eriyor ayazda.

Snow will fall
the death of my friend will be
the black shawl round my shoulders.

The dream begins with Deniz withdrawing.
In the dream a great garden,
and earth that smells of sleep in the garden.
I shall fix my eyes on the forest
and patience growing in my blood
will finally end.

Night saw it all.
Blood receding from the body,
the shrinking of the loins.
Whatever there was to murmur, was murmured to the moon.
I was left with a knife in my heart.
I look at leaves,
at my soul spoiled by the bitter taste in my mouth.
O deep gloomy desire whispered perhaps by the waters,

tread on the heart's dark stones, pass by on the other side.

People come into our lives and quietly leave.
Like a place slipping away
or perhaps like a tree stretching its branches.

When a deer is shot the body shudders
it is beauty's desire to live.

Darkness carries our destiny
and makes us feel.

If a phoenix appears in the coffee-grounds
it's a sign of rebirth. How I wish!
But rebirth will not happen.
Winter and a dark desire.
Snowfalls, a cheetah's bones
melt in the ice.

o şimdi içinde ormanın, çiçek dürbünü
ve ona bağışlanmış gözün ardına kadar açık oluşuyla.
boynumdaki boş muskaya dokundum.
sözün karnındaki yıkım ve gurura.

dönseydi,
ona dalların bedenleşmesini gösterecektim.
dil ve ruh kardeşti.

Şimdi gideceksin.
Orada bırakılmış kokusu var aşkın.
Bordo yatağında aşk uyuyacak.
Kapını açtığında eski aşk karşılayacak seni.
Bırakılmış aşk.

Bıçağı çeken inancı tazeledi.
İnsana ve tanrıya.
Bıçağı çeken kendini yok saydı kınında.

Büyük bir anıyla geçiyor aşk.
Bir ağaç gölgesinde beklenmiş
Ve baharlar ötesinden gelmemiş.
Bir yanılgının gövdemde seyirmesiyle hatırladım.
Gözleri karanlıktaydı onu ilk gördüğümde.
İki kuyu ve bir alna düşen duvar gölgesi.
Hepsi o kadar.

Bana ilk kez yaklaştığım o ormanda
Kaybetmeyi öğrettin.

She is in the forest now. Searching for flowers
with her kaleidoscopic gift of a wide-open eye.
I touched the empty amulet round my neck,
the pride and ruin within the word's belly.

If she returned
I would show her branches transformed into bodies.
Language and soul were sisters.

Now you will go.
Love's fragrance left there.
Love will sleep in your dark-red bed.
When you open your door old love will welcome you.
A love left behind.

Whoever drew the knife renewed his belief
in people and god.
Whoever drew the knife counted himself as nothing
in the sheath.

Love passes, great memories remain.
Awaited in the shadow of a tree,
far beyond spring it never comes.
With the tremor of error in my body
I remembered.
When I first saw him, his eyes were in darkness.
Two wells and a wall's shadow fell on a forehead.
That was all.

In that forest I first approached
you taught me loss.

BEJAN MATUR was born of an Alevi Kurdish family on 14 September 1968 in the ancient Hittite city of Maraş in southeast Turkey. Her first school was in her own village; later she attended the long-established Lycée in the region's most important cultural centre Gaziantep. These years were spent living with her sisters far from their parents. She studied Law at Ankara University, but has never practised. In her university years, she was published in several literary periodicals. Reviewers found her poetry "dark and mystic". The shamanist poetry with its pagan perceptions, belonging to the past rather than the present, of her birthplace and the nature and life of her village, attracted much attention. Her first book, *Rüzgar Dolu Konaklar*, published in 1996, unrelated to the contemporary mainstream of Turkish poets and poetry, won several literary prizes. Her second book, *Tanrı Görmesin Harflerimi* (1999) was warmly greeted. Two further books appeared at the same time in 2002, *Ayın Büyüttüğü Oğullar* and *Onun Çölünde*, continuing the distinctive language and world of imagery special to herself and her poetry.

Bejan Matur, who believes there is no frontier between poetry and life, travels the world like a long-term desert nomad. She stops by Istanbul, a city she sometimes lives in.

RUTH CHRISTIE was born and educated in Scotland, taking a degree in English Language and Literature at the University of St. Andrews. She taught for two years in Turkey and later studied Turkish language and literature at London University. For many years she taught English literature to American undergraduates resident in London. With Saliha Paker she translated a Turkish novel by Latife Tekin (Marion Boyars, 1993) and in collaboration with Richard McKane a selection of the poems of Oktay Rifat (Rockingham Press, 1993), and a major collection of Nâzım Hikmet's poetry, again with Richard McKane, was published by Anvil Press in 2002. Translations of several short stories and poems by other Turkish writers have appeared in magazines and anthologies in Britain and Turkey. At present, she and Richard McKane are completing a major collection of poems by Oktay Rifat, to be published by Anvil Press.

MAUREEN FREELY was born in Neptune, New Jersey, and grew up in Istanbul, Turkey. Since graduating from Harvard in 1974, she has lived mostly in England. She is the author of five novels – *Mother's Helper*, *The Life of the Party*, *The Stork Club*, *Under the Vulcania*, and *The Other Rebecca* – and three works of non-fiction. She is currently at work on a sixth novel – her second to be set in Istanbul. Her translation of Orhan Pamuk's *Snow* will be published by Faber in May 2004.

She is a senior lecturer in the Warwick Writing Programme in the Department of English at the University of Warwick. She is also a regular contributor to the *Times*, *Guardian*, *Observer*, *Sunday Times*, *Independent*, *New Statesman* and several Turkish magazines.